HURRICANE HUTCH'S
TOP 10 SHIPS OF THE CLYDE

By Captain Robin L Hutchison

As told to R D Dikstra

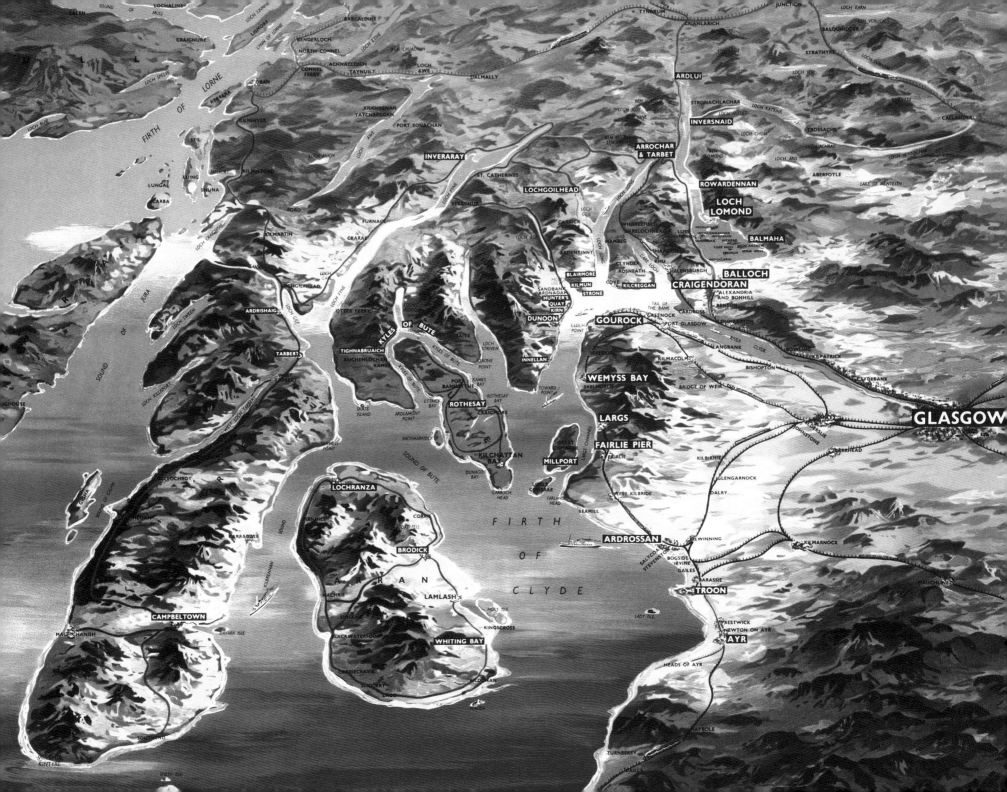

FOREWORD

This book is different from all the many others on Clyde Steamers. Most of those have been written by historians and steamer enthusiasts, but the author, Captain Robin Hutchison, is a retired Master Mariner. Although very much an enthusiast himself, he speaks from the perspective of one who served on the Clyde steamers. Robin was one of the most prominent of the post-war masters who served both on the traditional excursion steamers and the 'modern' car ferries dating from 1954. He was in post when The Caledonian Steam Packet Company joined with David MacBrayne Ltd to become Caledonian MacBrayne Ltd.

More important is the fact that Robin is an excellent story-teller with an eye for detail and a well-developed and gentle wit. The book contains many historical facts but they are told in a very 'un-stuffy' way and are laced with humour. What is important to Robin is life on board and to that end he tells how the officers and crews functioned on the different ships - in winter as well as summer and in heavy weather as well as calm seas. It is no accident that Captain Hutchison was known as 'Hurricane Hutch'!

Robin has been assisted in no small measure by his daughter Kay who has carried out all the necessary tasks in transforming the manuscript into a published book. The illustrations are from different sources, many through the Clyde River Steamer Club. All in all, this book is a must for all interested in the history of the Clyde steamers and ferries. The story is told by a man who knows his subject intimately and tells his story with great enthusiasm.

IAN MCCRORIE CalMac Historian

The Author on his 80th birthday

I remember waking up to the 'snick' of the snib closing on our front door as Dad quietly left for work. It would be five o'clock in the morning. Mum, Glenn and I were snug in our warm beds. Outside, it was pitch black and I would often lie there listening to the howling gales, rain lashing against the window. On those mornings, I wondered how on earth Dad would be able to sail in such conditions and continue to ferry his passengers safely across the water.

KAY HUTCHISON

First published in Great Britain in 2013 by Captain Robin L Hutchison/Belle Media Ltd

A Belle Media Book

ISBN Number 978-0-9927462-0-9

Design by Andrew Cook, es**sense** design

Printed in the UK by Fox Print

Published by Belle Media Ltd, London, UK
36/5 Ferry Lane, Ferry Quays, Brentford, Middlesex TW8 0AT
Tel +44 (0) 208 568 3556
www.bellemedia.co.uk

HURRICANE HUTCH'S
TOP 10 SHIPS OF THE CLYDE

As told to R D Dikstra

Belle Media, London

belle MEDIA

ACKNOWLEDGEMENTS

The following individuals and organisations helped
make this book possible.

Ian McCrorie | Kay Hutchison | Glenn Hutchison | Barry Dikstra

Hebridean Princess Cruises | Clyde River Steamer Club (CRSC) | Paddle Steamer Preservation Society

Caledonian MacBrayne | Ross Burridge | Steve Attridge | Greenock Telegraph | Jill Crookes

Sir Robert McAlpine | Sally Spencer | Anthony Williams

Watt Library, Inverclyde Council | Imperial War Museum

Friends of Wemyss Bay Station | Walter Bowie | Bryan Kennedy Collection

Aberdeen Maritime Museum | Michael Magnay | Miles Cowsill, Ferry Publications

A. Ernest Glen Collection, Camera on the Clyde

Robin Mills | Nicholas Leach, Ships Monthly | Eastern Daily Press

Bill Anderson, Dalrymple & Verdun Publishing

Gordon Rintoul, Director of National Museums of Scotland

National Railway Museum, Science & Society Picture Library

Glasgow Museums: Martin Bellamy, Emily Malcolm

Royal Commission of Ancient & Historical Monuments of Scotland

My grateful thanks,
Captain Robin L Hutchison

CONTENTS

INTRODUCTION

Captain on the *Maid of Argyll* Summer 1965

IN THIS BOOK I'VE TRIED TO GIVE YOU MY OWN PERSONAL TAKE ON A SLOWLY FADING ERA ON THE CLYDE. WHEN I FIRST STARTED WORK ON THE STEAMERS IT WAS IN THE LATE FIFTIES AND THE CALEDONIAN STEAM PACKET COMPANY'S SHIPS WERE STILL AN INTEGRAL PART OF LIFE FOR THE DOZENS OF COASTAL COMMUNITIES THAT HUGGED THE CLYDE ESTUARY. THE BOATS WERE BUILT TO CATER FOR A RANGE OF NEEDS. IN PEAK SEASON A CROWDED BOAT COULD HAVE UPWARDS OF 1,000 PASSENGERS ON BOARD.

A busy day cruising - *Waverley* and *Queen Mary II* near Colintraive July 1975 (CRSC)

Caledonian Isles battling the waves at Ardrossan (CRSC)

There were passengers commuting to and from the thriving industrial towns, there were people using the boats to reach their holiday destinations and those simply seeking a great day out. People sometimes fail to appreciate just how wide a social mix used our services. The well-to-do and the not-so-well-to-do all enjoyed using the boats and the ships therefore provided a mix of comfort, speed and affordability.

The boats ranged from the well-loved 'paddlers' to the more functional car ferries. One summer I ended up Master on eighteen different boats in twenty-one days, one minute handling paddlers, the next turbines and then on to the motor vessels, each with their own characteristics and idiosyncrasies. My rotas required me to join a new ship each day and meant me scurrying backwards and forwards between Adrossan, Ayr, Craigendoran, Gourock, Fairlie and Central Glasgow. I just about wore out a car trying to meet the schedules.

It's probably worth pointing out that we saw quite a difference between 'services' and 'cruises'. 'Services' were scheduled runs linking the towns and piers on the coast and strictly timetabled to connect with trains at different railheads. These trips were primarily about delivering people and goods to specific places at specific times; a vital mode of transportation to communities that depended upon us almost entirely. 'Cruises' on the other hand, were full or half-day excursions that allowed us some flexibility and gave people the opportunity to enjoy a relaxed day out on the river while also experiencing some of the finest scenery and freshest air in the country. During the peak summer months, the Company operated a complex timetable interweaving both types of sailings, and the boats might have to switch between roles several times during a single day. As time went by, however, this timetable was gradually modified to take account of the growing dominance of the car - and when I retired in 1995 it was from a CalMac that had become overwhelmingly a ferry service, shuttling cars and passengers from A to B. Its role and ethos had completely changed.

I had, however also now become part of an organization that dominated the sea routes of almost the entire West Coast of Scotland. We provided lifeline services to over 45 West Coast ports and island communities and indeed, by the time I retired, the Company was carrying some 5 million passengers and well over a million cars, commercial vehicles and coaches every year.

My time on the Clyde therefore bears witness to this transformation: on the one hand the gradual decline of the paddle steamer with its elegant dining saloons, linen tablecloths, silver cutlery, and genteel tea rooms, offering lazy summer cruises through stunning scenery; and on the other, the emergence of a fleet of powerful roll-on, roll-off car ferries capable of carrying the largest possible numbers of cars and commercial vehicles in the shortest possible time. But don't get me wrong, this is not simply a celebration of the past and a teary-eyed wallow in nostalgia. I enjoyed being in charge of the larger modern vessels like the four-and-a-half-thousand ton *Caledonian Isles* serving Arran and bringing in pioneering innovations such as Voith Schneider propulsion on the 'Streakers' (the nickname for a new class of vessel introduced in the early seventies). In many respects this was an exciting time of change.

My list of the Top 10 Ships of the Clyde is personal and it brings together all these disparate strands. It's from my own experience and intimate working knowledge of over thirty individual vessels and their crews that formed the Clyde fleet over some 35 years.

This book is about the Clyde as a living, breathing workplace.

My Seaman's Record Book

HURRICANE HUTCH

Aged 7 with mum and dad

I FIRST 'WENT TO SEA' IN 1942 AS AN ENTHUSIASTIC DECKHAND, AGED NINE - I WAS WORKING THE CREELS ON SMALL FISHING BOATS OUT OF DUNURE ON THE AYRSHIRE COAST WHILST ON MY HOLIDAYS. FROM THE OUTSET IT WAS OBVIOUS I REALLY ENJOYED BEING OUT ON THE WATER. MY PARENTS RAN A SMALL PRIVATE NURSING HOME FOR THE ELDERLY ON THE OUTSKIRTS OF GREENOCK AND WERE COMPLETELY TIED TO THE BUSINESS. GLENVILLE CATERED FOR ABOUT TWENTY-FIVE LONG-TERM PATIENTS, SO DURING THE YEAR MY PARENTS WERE ONLY ABLE TO TAKE A FEW ODD DAYS OFF HERE AND THERE.

My Seaman's Record Book begins with the *Hollypark* in 1950. The last entry is for the *Hebridean Princess*, May 1997

Fogarty Fegen's whistle - I kept it with me for over 40 years and it's still going strong.

Come the summer, I was usually packed off to my aunt's in Ayrshire for the holidays. As an only child I used to spend a lot of my time down at the harbour and got the opportunity to go out with the fishing boats almost every day. I sometimes got to steer, and was often told I had an instinctive feel for how to handle a boat. That summer, I even ended up going to the Isle of Man, talking my way on to a week-long trip across the Irish Sea. One of the fishermen had half-jokingly said, 'Want to come Hutchie?' and I immediately said 'YES!' It never occurred to me to ask anyone's permission, but I certainly got into trouble when I returned.

It was clear that the sea was in my blood. My mother was not so impressed, and was determined I would not become a fisherman. 'Poor as church mice', she would say, although, as far as I can remember, for much of the time, she was most definitely wrong about that: fishing was a very lucrative trade for most of the sixties and seventies. Anyway, a compromise was eventually struck and I left Greenock Academy at the ripe old age of fifteen to go to the James Watt Nautical College. After six months I set off for London as an apprentice with Denholm's. It was 1949. Before I left, one of the residents at the nursing home made a point of giving me a very special gift. She was the mother of Fogarty Fegen, the famous WWII Navy Captain who had gone down with his ship, HMS Jervis Bay, while trying to defend an Atlantic convoy. She presented me with her son's first officer's whistle. I think she felt proud to see a new generation go off to sea; even if it must have also brought back painful memories. It certainly meant a lot to me to have such a personal treasure as a reminder of home.

HMS *Jervis Bay* was an 'armed merchantman'- in reality just a lightly-armed converted cargo liner hastily pressed into naval service. In November 1940, she was the sole escort to a thirty-seven ship convoy carrying vital war supplies from Halifax, Nova Scotia to the UK. Single-handedly, the *Jervis Bay* was to take on the German 'pocket battleship', the *Admiral Scheer*. Completely outgunned by the heavily-armed German raider's six massive 11-inch guns, Captain Fegen was nonetheless determined to try everything he could to give the rest of the convoy as much time as possible to scatter and, hopefully, escape into the fast-gathering November darkness. His ship was hit multiple times, its guns destroyed, its bridge blown apart and Captain Fegen was himself gravely wounded, having lost an arm earlier in the battle. In a last desperate throw of the dice, he ordered his stricken vessel to turn directly towards the *Admiral Scheer* and tried to ram her at full speed. The *Jervis Bay* was sunk with the loss of one hundred and eighty-nine men before she got close enough, but the thirty-minute fight that she had put up in defence of the convoy proved vital in giving the other ships a chance to escape. In fact only four other ships in the convoy were sunk. The rest all got away, including the *San Demitrio*, a tanker carrying aviation fuel whose own exploits that night featured in a famous Ealing Studios propaganda film of the same name. The story of the *Jervis Bay* itself was partly the inspiration behind Alistair MacLean's first book HMS *Ulysses*. Captain Fegen was posthumously awarded the Victoria Cross - one of only twenty-three VC's awarded to the Royal Navy during the war. As the citation put it :-

'…challenging hopeless odds and giving his life to save the many ships it was his duty to protect'.

He was even mentioned by Churchill.

The war came quite close to us all at the nursing home. In those days, Glenville was out in the country on the road to Largs (it's all built-up now, of course). On the second night of the Greenock Blitz (7th May 1941) decoy flares were lit on the hills south of Greenock at Loch Thom and Flatterton to try to confuse the incoming bombers and draw them away from the town. The War Department wanted to make them think the fires on the open hillside were actually burning buildings on the ground. The strategy worked to some extent, with a number of bombs dropped on the hillside instead of the town, however it also brought us directly into the line of fire. One 1,000 lb parachute landmine floated down quite close to the house. Mother at first thought it was an enemy parachutist and stood at the upstairs bathroom window brandishing my father's 12 bore shot gun. Dad was out. He was an ARP Warden on 'fire watch'. Minutes earlier he had gone up the hill to try to put out incendiary bombs before

My first voyage on the *Hollypark* passing through Sydney Harbour Bridge 1950

they set fire to the local gun club hut. He was too late - he actually ended up lying face down in a ditch for over two hours, taking cover as best he could whilst bullets went flying everywhere as boxes of .303 ammunition exploded in the blaze.

Me? I was left 'guarding' the patients while we all sheltered in the downstairs hall cupboard.

The landmine landed about 60 feet away, in what was then an unloved, muddy field. Luckily, it had a delayed action fuse and only exploded after it had already sunk well into the bog.

Back home in Greenock with the dogs

At PS *Jupiter* ship's telegraph in 1956

The force of the explosion should have destroyed the house — possibly killing us all. Instead, it created a 30-ft-deep crater and threw up about three thousand tons of mud, most of which was splattered right across the entire front of Glenville. All the windows were blown in, most of the ceilings came down, and mother ended up in the bath. The only real casualty was her precious collection of antique china that was all but destroyed in the blast.

The patients had to be evacuated one by one, with a fleet of ambulances finally arriving some hours later. Two of the ambulances, in turn, ended up having to be rescued as they slid into the crater, patients and all, as the road itself was about a foot deep in soft mud. For some of the patients it was the second evacuation in 6 weeks, having only just been billeted on us from Clydebank, which had itself been bombed in March. Mum, Dad and I, however, just had to make do. We took shelter as best we could in what was still habitable, and my parents set about doing the repairs. All quite exciting for a seven-year-old but it must have been traumatic for everyone else. For a couple of weeks afterwards people came from miles around to see our 'lucky mud hut'.

I carried Fogarty Fegen's whistle with me throughout my 47-year career, and always felt proud to have even a small association with one of the Royal Navy's greatest heroes. It also served as a reminder of what so many of my own crewmates had themselves gone through in the War. Over the years I sailed with quite a number who had been torpedoed - some multiple times - and survived quite horrendous conditions.

My first ship was Denholm's SS *Hollypark*. I was to be paid the grand sum of £37 a year, and if I was to work more than ten hours in any one day I would be entitled to a massive one shilling and threepence (6p) an hour extra in overtime. In actual fact, despite the low pay, I managed to save quite a bit on that trip, as I was a keep-fit fanatic, and focused on my 'Charles Atlas' course. I kept out of trouble and was of course living 'all found' on board ship.

The *Hollypark* had been built to transport Sherman Tanks from the US during the war - she was originally known as the *Empire Tristram*. She was strongly built and, as it turned out, that was just as well. In late 1944, she was hit by a V1 flying bomb as she lay at her berth in London's Surrey Commercial Docks. Her sturdy construction meant she managed to survive the blast and was repaired. She was returned to the same docks a few months later, only to be hit a second time! The Germans seemed to have got her range. By the time I joined her five years later the *Hollypark* had been patched up quite successfully. Given that she had undertaken two enforced refits, she was better fitted out than most of the UK's remnant post-war merchant fleet, but the *Hollypark* was by no means luxurious. However, it did mean that we apprentices had our own individual cabins - something unheard of anywhere else at the time.

My first voyage was to Australia and New Zealand. I was supposed to be away for six months but due to a more-than-eventful trip, including being caught up in a seven-month dock strike marooned in Picton, New Zealand, I finally returned to Greenock, some twenty five months later, aged eighteen. I'd had to grow up quickly. My father had died while I was away but it was simply not practical for me to return - the voyage home would have taken me a minimum of six weeks – so I just had to make the best of the situation and get on with it, twelve thousand miles from home. I got on well with the crew on the *Hollypark* and learnt quickly. Normally it took at least four years to make 3rd Mate but I was promoted on my very next trip on the *Hollypark*, with my salary racing ahead to a handsome £31.2s.6d a month (£31.12p), more than ten times what I had previously earned as an apprentice. I thought I was a millionaire!

For the next six years I was 'deep sea', with trips to South & Central America, Australia, The Great Lakes, Panama & Suez Canals, the Middle East, Cape Horn, Tierra del Fuego, the Mediterranean and even Siberia.

Two incidents perhaps best illustrate the times and the places we sailed to :-

Firstly, Christmas of 1953, I was 3rd Mate on the SS *Gleddoch*, an ore carrier in La Goulette, the main port in what was then French Tunisia. This was around the time of the Tunisian and Algerian struggles for independence. One of my duties in preparing the ship for departure was to make a full inspection to discover possible stowaways. I went up to the boat deck and lifted the tarpaulin covering one of the lifeboats on the port side and came face to face with a large, shaven-headed German – clearly a deserter from the Foreign Legion. He looked at me with terrified eyes, swore loudly (or so I assumed) and immediately jumped out on to the deck and fled toward the gangway. Just as he got to the bottom of the gangway I heard multiple shots rapidly ring out and saw him slump, almost cut in half by the bullets fired from the dockside by two of his fellow Legionnaires. No mercy there, just a brutal iron discipline. Oddly, after all these years, I still vividly remember the three baguettes he had sticking out of his pockets as he ran - all the food

My walk-on part in CalMac's publicity campaign - taken on board the
Sannox in the early 80s

he had managed to scavenge for his desperate and ultimately futile escape attempt. Very sad.

The other incident was at Poti on Georgia's Black Sea coast in 1958 - a time of considerable East-West tensions. It was on the MV *Clarkavon*, another ore carrier. In the process of docking I suddenly saw one of the steel wires attached to the main ropes come under unexpected tension and called 'Look out! That's going to go', pointing at the capstan and the wire. In an instant, there was a loud snapping and a great whooshing noise and the wire whipped across the deck and caught my outstretched finger, breaking it instantly. I was in agony and needed urgent medical attention. The most obvious place to get it was ashore, but it took five hours of security questioning before the authorities were willing to actually allow me off the ship. Even then I have to say the attention was rudimentary. They did reset the finger, but without much skill and without anaesthetic - exceedingly painful as I can recall even after nigh on sixty years. And the finger? Well, it's still twisted to this day.

Throughout the fifties, I was mainly 'deep sea', but after that first prolonged trip out to New Zealand, I was able to return home on leave fairly frequently. Like so many others, I used to go to the dancing on a Saturday night at the Moorings in Largs. There I met my future wife Ann. Gradually the pull of a proper home life meant I began to work summer seasons on the Clyde with CalMac's predecessor The Caledonian Steam Packet Company (CSPC). Every summer during the late fifties, they ran no fewer than 19 ships on the Clyde; such was the demand. Consequently, they took on a considerable number of experienced summer season staff. Out of season, I was free to return to deep sea or to coastal UK work. There was no shortage of work available for someone with my experience.

Eventually, in late 1962, and after three summer seasons with the CSPC, I was lucky enough to get offered a full time position on the Clyde. I was to start mid-January and that meant I had to turn down an alternative offer from MacCallum's, as Mate on the *Ardgarry*. Only a month later, I heard that she had sunk on that very voyage, just before New Year off the Scilly Isles in a Force 11 storm with the loss of all twelve crew - something that has stayed with me all these years. This is the reality of life at sea and as it happens, I got the nickname Hurricane Hutch for what seemed to be my uncanny knack of being on duty whenever the weather worsened. An almost magnetic power of attraction between me and 15-foot waves, or so it seemed. In those days, however, we always tried to keep the services running whenever we could. We understood that people on the islands depended on us so, that said, my crews had frequent experience of the full power of the sea in bad weather - and a strong wish they could be somewhere else.

The sea's ability to change from glassy smooth to raging torrent is part of its unique fascination, and I suppose the reason why sailors the world over have a unique bond of friendship whenever they meet. This is also why I can look back on my time with such fond regard, despite the long hours, the rough weather and the relatively poor pay. Yes, the Clyde is about magnificent scenery and picturesque little seaside towns, but in harsh weather the waters can be brutal.

I hope you enjoy my Top 10, I certainly enjoyed putting it together.

ONE MV MAID OF ARGYLL

Maid of Argyll in gusty conditions off Gourock 1968 (CRSC)

THE MAID OF ARGYLL WAS PROBABLY MY FAVOURITE SHIP. SHE WAS A PURPOSE-BUILT PASSENGER FERRY COMMISSIONED IN 1953 AS PART OF AN ONGOING PROCESS OF POST-WAR MODERNISATION. IT WAS ONE OF FOUR SIMILAR VESSELS - THE MAIDS OF ASHTON, ARGYLL, SKELMORLIE AND CUMBRAE. ALL WERE BUILT ON THE CLYDE TO THE SAME SPECIFICATION IN THE SAME YEAR AND TWO WERE EVEN BUILT IN THE SAME SHIPYARD. BUT THEY WERE ALL DIFFERENT...

Maid of Argyll August 1969 dodging the yachts on a beautiful sunny day - Culture and Sport Glasgow (Glasgow Museums)

My 1961 copy of the Clyde Pilots' Handbook detailing every fact and figure regarding navigation on the river.

The *Maid of Ashton* was built at Yarrow's, the *Maids of Argyll* and *Skelmorlie* by A&J Inglis in Glasgow, and the *Maid of Cumbrae* at Ardrossan Dockyard. Despite a shared design it always amazed me how very differently each handled when at sea. Ultimately, when it came down to it, the actual manufacture of ships on the Clyde in the fifties still retained a substantial element of individual, traditional hand-built craft skills. I suppose that is also partly why each vessel had its own unique personality.

The *Argyll* was undoubtedly the best and the most responsive of the four *Maids*. It was also the first ship on which I became Master and in those days the Company required officers to have served at least ten years on the Clyde before becoming Master – though I managed it in nine. No wonder this, my first command, was always close to my heart.

Masters, by the way, also needed to have a Clyde Pilot's Licence, which basically meant you knew the River like the back of your hand. To get your licence you had to 'do your time' (measured in years). There was also an oral examination that you had to pass to prove to the Pilotage Authorities that you knew virtually every rock and shoal on the five hundred square miles of the Clyde from the southernmost tip of Arran, right up to the very heart of Glasgow. You had to know the courses, buoy-to-buoy, for the twenty-two miles from the Cumbrae Heads, where the Estuary officially stops and the Clyde becomes a river, right up to Bridge Wharf in the heart of Glasgow: the place where commercial navigation ceases.

The *Maid of Argyll* was designed for regular passenger services. She provided the daily 10 am weekday service from Craigendoran to Rothesay, connecting with the train from

Glasgow and calling at the intermediate piers of Gourock, Dunoon and Innellan. The return service arrived back at Craigendoran in the early afternoon. Often, on top of this, we might have an evening cruise to do as well, finishing work just before midnight. On the weekends we took over the 'Three Lochs' trips from the *Waverley*, so that her larger passenger-carrying capacity could be used on extended trips to Rothesay.

An unheralded but vital additional 'ghost' service was the eight o'clock 'Bun Run' from Gourock to Craigendoran. Every morning, come rain or shine, thousands of sausage rolls, fondant fancies, empire biscuits, coconut slices, cream doughnuts and mini apple tarts were transported over from CalMac's own bakery on Gourock pier. The bakery was a major part of CalMac's operation back then, and at one stage it employed over one hundred people in its efforts to 'feed the ships'. Different boats were used for the bun run depending on availability and not all of them were totally suitable: but it was principally a task for one of the *Maids*. The large wooden baker's boards that we used to transport the cakes were often simply laid out across the seating on the open decks, and more than one crafty seagull got away with a delicious creamy doughnut. Perhaps only in the West of Scotland could you imagine a dedicated 'bun boat' being carefully timetabled as a vital element of a day's maritime operations.

Craigendoran was quite a shallow pier, and it really only kept open through the constant churning up of the water from the comings and goings of the four boats based there and the twice-daily tidal flows. Nowadays, it's silted up and you probably couldn't get a rowing boat near it. So, perhaps not a natural choice for one of the principal harbours on the Clyde:

Maid of Argyll July 1964 - Culture and Sport Glasgow (Glasgow Museums)

The 'Bun Run' - buns, cakes and sausage rolls from Cal Mac's own Bakery, Gourock Pier circa 1960

Maid of Argyll at Craigendoran (CRSC)

the story goes that it was chosen as a railhead pier simply to keep the Glasgow 'oiks' from sullying the genteel streets of Helensburgh. Whatever the reason, it was a pier to be wary of on a ship like the *Argyll*. It was perfectly manageable for the traditional paddle steamers, with their relatively shallow draft and their side paddles skimming the surface water, but the propeller-driven *Maids* were more tricky.

Approaching the pier, you had to slow the ship almost to a stop half-a-mile out, otherwise the propellers would create a trough in the water immediately behind the boat as a result of their running in too shallow water. In turn this trough would be back-filled by a powerful following wave, which would then build as you went along. This following wave would eventually catch you up and hit the boat on the stern just as you came alongside: this additional 'push' was strong enough to break the strongest mooring ropes - extremely dangerous - so a cautious approach was always essential.

FACT SHEET

- Built: 1953, A & J Inglis, Glasgow
- Entered service: 1953
- Left service: 1973
- Length: 161 ft
- Tonnage: 508 tons
- Speed: 15 kts
- Capacity: 627 passengers

VIEW FROM THE BRIDGE

As I said, although regular river services were the norm, we also did cruises. The Kyles of Bute was a favourite. Tighnabruaich must be one of the most beautifully situated piers in the country, with the purple hills falling gently down to the little picturesque town lying at the water's edge. It's no wonder the Kyles have a special place in so many hearts.

One time, the Purser came up to tell me a family wanted to scatter the ashes of a loved one in the middle of the channel. These requests were quite frequent - at least once a week - and most Captains tried to accommodate them whenever possible. The Kyles, however, are narrow and you could not afford to slow down for too long, especially if the wind was blowing strongly. On this occasion I could see that the family were already gathered near the stern and, as was common practice, they had asked one of the sailors, to quietly 'do the business'. He would scatter the ashes whilst they gathered round the Minister for a short prayer. Sailors liked the task. Not only did they see it as a welcome break from the routine, but also they could expect to be rewarded with a drop of 'hospitality' immediately afterwards, in the downstairs bar. Sometimes drink was taken ahead of the committal, given the long sail out to the Kyles. I suspect this particular day was one such occasion…

Heading through the Kyles there was quite a strong following wind, and I knew I could only slow for a minute or two or she would be on the rocks. As the boat slowed, I signalled with my cap to the minister that he should begin. Imagine my consternation when, as the minister began, I saw, almost in slow motion, a sailor walk slowly to the stern rail, solemnly lift the lid of the ornate copper casket and, exactly on cue, cast the ashes seaward…right into the following wind!

The mourning group tried as best they could to maintain some degree of composure, a few even had to stifle their own embarrassed laughter as they brushed themselves down, minister included, and wiped the ashes from their eyes. The sailor all-too-quickly returned the casket to the minister and retreated giving a little bow, apparently remembering more pressing duties elsewhere. I shook my head - I couldn't believe it - and turned back to bring the *Argyll* up to cruising speed and back on course for Craigendoran.

SHIP'S LOG

The *Maid of Argyll* was withdrawn in 1973 after twenty years' service. She was sold to a Greek shipping company, becoming the *City of Piraeus*. Boats on the Clyde were worked hard, so at least it's nice to think that she enjoyed a few years of retirement in the sun sailing the Aegean, before her demise as the *City of Corfu* after a serious fire.

Maid of Argyll off Dunoon Summer 1961 (CRSC)

With my wife Ann and Glenn at Millport in the late 60s

Maid of Argyll burnt out at Kerkyra, Corfu in 1997. Note the embossed *Piraeus* painted over and the name *Corfu* roughly added in blue - suggests an uncared-for final season (Bryan Kennedy)

TWO TS QUEEN MARY II

Queen Mary II leaving Largs, June 1967 (CRSC)

THE QUEEN MARY II WAS QUITE SIMPLY A MAGNIFICENT CRUISING SHIP: A REAL PLEASURE TO BE ON, BOTH AS PASSENGER OR CREW. BEAUTIFULLY PLANNED BY EXPERIENCED SAILORS AND STEWARDS - PEOPLE WHO ACTUALLY HAD TO USE THE VESSEL DAY-IN AND DAY-OUT. IT HAD CLEAN LINES, GENEROUS PASSENGER ACCOMMODATION AND GOOD DECK-SPACE. TO MY MIND SHE WAS THE ONLY BOAT IN THE ENTIRE COMPANY THAT THE MANAGEMENT HADN'T HAD A CHANCE TO INTERFERE WITH WHEN SHE WAS BEING DESIGNED AND IT REALLY SHOWED.

The *Queen Mary* in 1934 with her original two funnels passing the as-yet-unnamed Hull 534 at John Brown's Shipyard in Clydebank - she was renamed *Queen Mary II* later that year and then in 1957 was converted to a single funnel.
Culture and Sport Glasgow (Glasgow Museums)

Three generations of CalMac - *Queen Mary II, Glen Sannox* and hovercraft,
Rothesay 1970

As a turbine steamer she was quiet, smooth and very fast. When she launched in 1933 (the year I was born) she was simply known as the *Queen Mary*. She became the *Queen Mary II* a year later when Cunard / White Star wanted to use the name for their famous liner RMS *Queen Mary*. I grew up with one story about the naming that always intrigued me. Initially the Cunard-White Star ship was simply known as 'Hull No 534'.

During the Depression, work stopped, and for two years the 534's massive unfinished frame became a powerful symbol of idleness and unemployment on the Clyde. Consequently, when work finally recommenced, it was seen as a real symbol of hope and there was considerable public interest in its launch, as well as great speculation about its naming. It seems the owners had originally intended to name it the *Queen Victoria*. However, or so the story goes, when they told Buckingham Palace that they intended to name the ship after 'Britain's greatest Queen', King George V simply responded that 'my wife would be delighted at such an honour'. With a response like that it seemed there was absolutely no option but to comply - *Queen Mary* it was. And therefore our wee boat had to play second fiddle. Whatever the truth, it certainly caused considerable confusion on the Clyde for the next 40 years.

Our *Queen Mary* dropped the 'II' suffix in 1976, and reverted to her original name when Cunard's RMS *Queen Mary* was finally pensioned off to become a floating hotel complex in Long Beach, California. Now of course, just to add insult to injury in what has become a very complex story, Cunard has a new 150,000 ton *Queen Mary 2* sailing (it should be 3), and she's no stranger to the Clyde either. However, real Clyde enthusiasts know there has only ever been one *Queen Mary II*.

On the Clyde in her final season (Michael Magnay)

Dining on the *Jeanie Deans* – the *Queen Mary II* was a cut above - Culture and Sport Glasgow (Glasgow Museums)

Queen Mary II at Erskine Bridge heading towards Glasgow, Summer 1971 (CRSC)

FACT SHEET

- Built: 1933, Denny, Dumbarton
- Entered service: 1933
- Left service: 1977
- Length: 253 ft
- Tonnage: 1,014 tons
- Speed: 20 kts
- Capacity: 1,820 passengers

VIEW FROM THE BRIDGE

I was Mate for most of my time on the *Queen Mary II*. In those days she was mainly manned by what we called the 'summer-time teuchters': all experienced seafarers down from the Western Isles for the summer season. For all my time with CalMac, these islanders made up a significant proportion of the crews and helped give the ships a uniquely friendly feel.

On the *Queen Mary II* every sailor had his own 'wee croft', their own wee piece of ground, a special patch of the boat for which he was personally responsible. He looked after it as if it were his own property, constantly polishing the brass and cleaning the paintwork. Each crewman was really proud of his own wee area and deeply embarrassed if, on inspection, you ever found fault. This communal pride in the condition of the boat was one of the things that made her such a pleasure to be on.

A sail would not be complete without a visit to the Dining Saloon. Full silver service, starched white linen, efficiency and good quality food were all hallmarks of a trip on the *Queen Mary II*.

The ship was based at Bridge Wharf in Glasgow and in those days the city was extremely industrial - the 'Second City of the Empire' with shipyards as far as the eye could see: docks, iron foundries, printing works, carpet factories, chemical and dye works; a constant industrial machine pounding away night and day and all discharging their waste into the Clyde. The *Queen Mary II* lay at her berth on the southern side of the river, right in the heart of the city and directly opposite the Broomielaw. Every night, as the general roar of city-centre life gradually stilled, you could hear the toxic gases rising from the industrial silt of the riverbed below, and gently bubbling upwards to break the surface.

One morning, I remember the Chief Steward going ballistic when he went into the Dining Room and discovered that the night before one of the Assistant Stewards had forgotten to close one of the porthole windows. Overnight, a thousand pieces of silver cutlery and silver plate that had been meticulously cleaned, polished and laid out on the starched white linen tablecloths ready for the next day's passengers, had turned a nasty dark brown. Whatever it was that was bubbling from the depths of the river I would not like to think, but it certainly was powerful. I had physically to hold the Chief Steward back from killing the poor lad. There was no option but for the whole catering staff to abandon their normal duties and set to work to rescue the situation, cleaning and polishing every single piece once again from scratch. Needless to say by the time we were ready to sail at 10 am the entire Saloon was once more at its gleaming best, and the boys knew they had better never, ever repeat that mistake.

Aerial view of *Queen Mary II*, Summer 1971 (CRSC)

Laid up at East India Harbour, Greenock in 1978 in CalMac livery - she had been renamed *Queen Mary* in 1976 following the retirement of Cunard's RMS *Queen Mary* (Michael Magnay)

SHIP'S LOG

The *Queen Mary II* made her last trip on the Clyde at the end of the Summer Season of 1977 and eventually, after a four-year lay-up in Greenock, was sold to become a floating restaurant on the Thames. In 2009, she was again sold and there was talk of her becoming a restaurant in the Atlantic port and holiday resort of La Rochelle, France - but the recession intervened. She was subsequently towed away from her berth, and taken to Tilbury to await her future.

In 1987, now with a double funnel and uninspiring colour scheme, *Queen Mary* reappears on the Thames to begin her stint as a floating restaurant (Bryan Kennedy)

THREE MV COWAL

Cowal 1968 - Culture and Sport Glasgow (Glasgow Museums)

DESPITE LACKING THE ELEGANCE OF THE 'PADDLERS', THE COWAL WAS A GREAT SHIP WITH A GREAT CREW. SHE ALSO REPRESENTED THE SHEER VARIETY OF WHAT THE CLYDE HAD TO OFFER IN THE SIXTIES. A SINGLE DAY'S DUTY COULD SEE US BREAK OFF FROM THE REGULAR WEMYSS BAY TO MILLPORT RUN IN ORDER TO GO AND PICK UP LIVESTOCK ON A SPECIAL CHARTER AND ENDING THE DAY ON A COMMUTER/CAR FERRY RUN, BUT THIS TIME TO DUNOON AND BACK TO GOUROCK.

The *Cowal* at Rothesay Pier, October 1969 (CRSC)

An Armstrong Siddeley Sapphire driving off the *Cowal's* hydraulic car lift at Gourock in her first season in 1954. (Photograph by A. Ernest Glen from 'Camera on the Clyde')

FACT SHEET

- Built: Ailsa Yard, Troon, Ayrshire
- Entered service: 1954
- Left service: 1977
- Length: 179 ft
- Tonnage: 569 tons
- Speed: 14 kts
- Capacity: 650 passengers, 34 cars
- Vehicle handling: side loading, hydraulic lift from car deck to dockside

The *Cowal* was one of three similar vessels (the others were the *Arran* and the *Bute*) collectively known as 'ABCs' that were built as a first response to the post-war boom in car traffic. The ships heralded a new era - the beginning of the public's long love affair with the car. But they also presaged a time when the simple pleasures of cruising down the Clyde would begin to lose out to the lure of guaranteed sun and cheap living on the 'Costas'. The ABCs also showed that the Company had much to learn about how demand was actually changing. The designs were somewhat of a compromise between our traditional passenger-only vessels and out-and-out car ferries. That said, they were capable of cruising the Clyde in reasonable comfort with up to 650 passengers, and still transporting up to 34 cars and passengers to Rothesay or Dunoon.

Car handling, however, was a problem. In the early fifties no-one foresaw the growth in demand for car ferries on the Clyde, and neither the Company, nor the various local authorities involved, wanted to pay to provide the costly, variable height, linkspans needed to cope with the tidal movements at each pier. Instead, the ABCs used a compromise solution using on-board hydraulic hoists to line up with the pier side each time they berthed. Loading and unloading were therefore rather complex operations.

Cars had to be driven on to the car hoists at the stern, then rotated 90 degrees using the revolving turntables embedded on the hoist floor, lowered, and finally driven off and along the car/cargo deck that ran the length of the ship. Each vehicle then had to be rotated again on the bow turntable, ready to drive back to the hoist, to reverse the procedure when finally offloaded at their destination. The use of hoists and turntables might have been a clever technical solution when first proposed in planning meetings in a nice cosy office (and at a time when traffic forecasts were quite low), but they proved much more challenging in real life when you are trying to keep up an hourly schedule on the Clyde in all weathers. Side loading also limited a ship's ability to take large commercial vehicles - and this was to be a constant source of criticism.

The *Cowal's* crew, however, really gelled and were exceptionally well drilled. Even with a full complement of 34 cars we managed to get our turn round times down to ten minutes – Formula 1 pit crews probably couldn't have done better. Sandy Stevenson was the real expert - you could always rely on him to shift the queue.

VIEW FROM THE BRIDGE

I was originally Mate, eventually becoming Master. The first skipper of the *Cowal* was 'Big Bad' John MacLeod and I think everyone agreed he ran a very efficient ship. He had a great crew, but when he lost his temper, trust me, you didn't want to be there!

The limitations on vehicle handling meant big lorries were difficult to accommodate, and so when it came to transporting livestock from Arran, Bute or Cumbrae the animals were usually simply carried loose on the car deck on special sailings. On many an occasion I've known the whole car deck, bow to stern, taken up with a sea of sheep. On the one hand, these sailings could be quite a headache for us but, on the other, the island's farmers saw it all as a bit of a day's jolly. They would usually be ready at the dockside, bright and early, hours before we were due, spending the intervening time in a friendly local hostelry - a chance to chat to their fellow farmers, complain about prices and moan about the weather. As a result, by the time loading began, it was often left to our crew to cope with the animals on their own, with the farmers simply standing about half gassed, while passing on the odd word of encouragement.

I remember more than one runaway bull careering towards the high street in Rothesay, closely followed by two or three able seamen in hot pursuit, and with the odd surprised bystander having to dart quickly into a nearby shop - the farmers themselves nowhere to be seen. Luckily, we always got them back, even if it sometimes required the help of the local police.

The farmers usually travelled with us to 'supervise' things at the other side, but as you might expect, by the time we got to the mainland the situation was no better. Even though we had no

Off Toward, approaching Rothesay July 1973 (Anthony Williams)

Mail and Milk being off-loaded at Gourock 1954. (Photograph by A. Ernest Glen from 'Camera on the Clyde')

Cowal August 1969 - Culture and Sport Glasgow (Glasgow Museums)

other passengers, the Company treated it as a normal sailing and so the ship's bar was fully staffed and open for business from the moment we left the pier.

Needless to say the crew became experts in livestock handling and the car deck got a good hosing down each trip ready for the next sailing.

At times, life on board was more hazardous than it should have been. Once, on the *Cowal's* sister ship the *Bute*, I was passing the galley on my way back from checking on a capstan that needed tightening every four or five berthings. I noticed the cook looking blankly at some sausages he was frying. Where the Company got those people from I do not know, but as far as I could see this must have been a boy they just picked up off the street: he certainly didn't seem to have had any training. The sausages were for the crew's dinner, but they were turning white instead of golden brown and the 'cook', it seemed, didn't have a clue what to do. It didn't give me much confidence when I saw that the sausages were still all linked together and coiled around in the pan.

I also noticed a rather funny, but familiar smell - antifreeze!

Evidently the boy had used a half-opened plastic container marked 'Cooking Oil' that he had found in the back of the galley. It was actually a gallon of antifreeze. It turned out the helmsman had bartered with a Fire Service mechanic travelling over from Dunoon (for God knows what) and he had stored the antifreeze in the first receptacle that came to hand and hidden it - or at least so he thought. Unfortunately our new 'cook' had come across it, ignored the funny smell and colour and simply got on with the frying. Thankfully I stopped him killing us. However, only five minutes later when I popped back to check how things were, I was completely astonished to discover that the very same sausages were now being carefully rinsed under the tap. He was feeding the links like a rope into the giant stainless steel sink. I ensured that he started again from scratch. Recruitment and training practices have hopefully improved over the years since.

SHIP'S LOG

Gradually overtaken by more modern purpose-built car ferries, the *Cowal* was eventually withdrawn from service in mid-1977. Some years later, she was sold to Greek shipping interests, but never actually went back into service and was broken up in 1984.

FOUR PS CALEDONIA

A new dawn - *Caledonia* refitting after war service, Dumbarton 1945 - Culture and Sport Glasgow (Glasgow Museums)

THE CALEDONIA WAS PROBABLY THE FINEST SEA BOAT OF THE PRE-WAR FLEET AND GOOD IN BAD WEATHER - A MAJOR BOON ON THE CLYDE EVEN IN HIGH SUMMER. PADDLE STEAMERS HAVE A REAL CHARM, BUT THEY ALSO HAVE ONE KEY VULNERABILITY: BREAKING A BLADE. WHEN THE CLYDE SHIPYARDS WERE IN FULL FLOW AND LOOSE CARGOES WERE STILL BEING LOADED AND UNLOADED IN THE DOCKS, FLOATING WOOD AND DEBRIS IN THE RIVER WAS A MAJOR PROBLEM.

Caledonia in May 1962 (CRSC)

Even today with the shipyards all but disappeared and the benefits of containerisation, a lot of debris still floats on or just below the surface of the Clyde. On the *Caledonia*, breaking a paddle was not just a problem, it could be potentially disastrous as she had steel blades.

I remember when I was Mate, reversing out of Millport once when she lost a blade on her starboard side. The broken blade had actually torn right through the wooden paddle box housing and landed out on the main deck - it could have caused someone a very nasty injury. It was only luck that the boat was quiet and nobody was nearby. With a blade missing, the paddles couldn't turn. We were helpless. The design of the paddle wheel is actually quite complex - one key component is the wonderfully named 'Jenny Nettles', part of the damping mechanism on the paddle wheel that is designed to feather the blades when they enter the water. A missing blade unbalanced the whole mechanism, so a broken paddle meant we had no option but to drop anchor and await rescue.

The *Glen Sannox* initially had to divert up from Arran to tow us out of the channel into deep water where we anchored again until such time as one of the tugs based at Greenock could come out and take us back home. A tug, the *Campaigner*, duly arrived. Unfortunately, after quickly getting the tow-rope attached, the tug set off for Greenock a little too enthusiastically. A broken paddle wheel needs to be held firmly in place to avoid further damage as the ship moves through the water. Mistakenly the engineers had thought that the broken blade itself had jammed the wheel and saw no need to independently chain it down. The force of the water as we moved along at full speed however was enough to dislodge the broken pieces, and the unbalanced wheel started spinning in the water and disintegrated under the strain, causing yet more delay. A frustrating, expensive and disruptive process and all caused from simply hitting a bit of driftwood.

Actually, Millport was a bit of a jinxed destination for the *Caley* - I can remember coming from Brodick one summer's day in a howling gale (yes, I did say summer) and nearly going ashore on Little Cumbrae. We had 400 passengers on board, had crossed the firth and were coming up on the east side of the island. We had increased our speed to 10 knots as the wind raged, but when we passed the cliffs the wind changed, suddenly just taking her: we didn't have enough forward speed to get her back under control. We had to urgently ring for more speed as the boat was being forced ashore. Jimmy Simpson was Captain and in desperation he was shouting down the brass speaking tube to Tommy the Engineer,

'More speed, more speed!!'

The engineer rushed to open up the throttles and get the revs up to the absolute max but paddle steamers are not instantly responsive. We kept lurching ever closer to the shore. Jimmy kept calling down more and more desperately until all we could do was pray. Finally, with the engine shuddering, we gained some control of her and narrowly avoided disaster.

The Clyde has some tricky areas to navigate and that incident helped emphasize the need to always have some power in reserve when conditions suddenly change.

Somehow paddle steamers and their engines always go hand in hand: nowhere else do you go and see engines on a vessel as a matter of course on open display. And a visit to the engines was always an exciting highlight of any trip on board a paddle steamer. Raw power located right at the centre of the ship but fully open to view - something you simply don't see now apart from on the *Waverley*. Passengers loved watching the enormous gleaming pistons and interconnected crankshafts rhythmically and noisily pounding away in the oppressive heat. They also delighted in hearing the ding, ding of instructions relayed down from the bridge on the traditional ship's telegraph.

The *Caledonia's* engine room perimeter was entirely coated in a uniform creamy gloss paint, probably ten layers deep, and giving the whole place a soft ethereal feel. The engines themselves: the noise, the bright shiny motion and the hot oily smells, must have been an inspiration for countless wee boys to pursue a career in engineering. 'I'm just going down to take a look at the engines' was also a popular euphemism for a quick visit to the bar and many a child must have thought the fumes awfully strong down there when their father finally emerged from his visit down below, a little unsteady on his feet.

A glamorous night out in 60s Millport

Caledonia Engine Room (CRSC)

Busy gangways on Fair Monday

FACT SHEET

- Paddle steamer
- Built: 1934, Denny, Dumbarton
- Entered service: 1934
- Left service: 1969
- Length: 224 ft
- Tonnage: 623 tons
- Speed: 15 kts
- Capacity: 1,730 passengers

VIEW FROM THE BRIDGE

The *Caledonia* was usually based in Ayr for the summer season and I spent five summers there. We did cruises to several destinations including the Kyles, Arran and Campbeltown.

It's difficult now to convey to people the sheer popularity of Clyde Cruising, the masses of people who used the boats, and the complex interlinked timetable of services and cruises we offered. In high summer, well over 15,000 people could be sailing on the Clyde on our ships at any one time. Incredible when you think of it. One story perhaps helps illustrate just how busy it was.

It was mid-July - the height of the Glasgow Fair holiday - and there were easily 1,200 people on board, with the main promenade deck packed with sun-seekers. We were just leaving Dunoon when two little old ladies approached me. 'Does this boat go to Millport, Captain?' 'No', I replied, 'you'll need to change at Largs, but don't worry, it's an easy connection. Board the boat lying ahead of us at the pier and she'll take you over'.

Simple. Or so I thought.

As we headed into Largs, sure enough, and just as I had expected, the *Talisman* was already alongside the pier and awaiting the connection with us. There were easily 250 people jam-packed on the dockside eagerly waiting to rush on and try to grab a seat on deck. On glancing to the rear, I also estimated we had about a hundred passengers wanting to get off at Largs - including

Caledonia August 1969 - Culture and Sport Glasgow (Glasgow Museums)

the little old ladies. As always on busy summer days, we used two gangways: the forward one for boarding and the aft for disembarking passengers. Keeping to schedule mattered and so, no more than five minutes later, we were steaming off once more, now heading non-stop for Ayr.

Walking through the tea room I was surprised to see one of the ladies still there. She came up to me and said, 'Why didn't you tell us you were coming on this boat too, Captain?' I didn't know what to say… they were obviously on the wrong boat. I could only imagine they had been swept off our rear gangway with the disembarking crowds. Unable to see much in the throng, instead of making their way on to the *Talisman* as I had directed, they must have been carried along in the general melee, and swept back up onto our forward gangway, together with all the other new passengers that had been waiting for us on the pier. They were back aboard, precisely where they had started. And still headed for Ayr…

SHIP'S LOG

Over the years the crowds vanished, and the *Caledonia* was withdrawn in 1969. Some believe she would have been a better example of a Clyde Steamer to preserve than the *Waverley* (and my ranking of her as my top 'paddler' bears that out), but it was not to be. The *Caledonia* ended her days on the Thames as a floating restaurant. I visited her just the once on the Embankment and although it was rather sad to see her marooned like that, it was fascinating to realise that even on a static mooring on the Thames they were not able to cure her list to port. Fire eventually got her, and in mid-1980 she was scrapped.

Caledonia approaching Gourock August 1967 - Culture and Sport Glasgow (Glasgow Museums)

FIVE MV JUPITER

Jupiter at Dunoon in 1977 - Culture and Sport Glasgow (Glasgow Museums)

THE JUPITER WAS THE FIRST OF THE 'STREAKERS' - THEY WERE POWERFUL, EXTREMELY VERSATILE AND HIGHLY MANOEUVRABLE SHIPS. THE VOITH SCHNEIDER, VARIABLE-PITCH PROPULSION MEANT THEY COULD TURN IN THEIR OWN LENGTH, GO SIDEWAYS AND, ON ONE MEMORABLE OCCASION, I EVEN DEMONSTRATED THEIR ABILITY TO BEAT OUR RIVALS WHILST GOING ASTERN!

The *Jupiter* and her sister ships *Juno* and *Saturn* were designed to replace the ABC car ferries that had first come in to service in the early fifties. The growth in car traffic demanded a new approach in both ship and pier design. The powers that be eventually agreed to provide the variable linkspans at each pier, although it was only a compromise, as it still required side loading at both Dunoon and Rothesay. This ruled out a full roll-on roll-off approach to the design of the ships. The Streakers performed the compromise position admirably, enabling us to carry a full range of commercial traffic and halving our all-important turnaround times.

I brought the *Jupiter* out new from Lamont's in Port Glasgow in 1974. The Streakers were unique amongst all of the ships using Voith propulsion at that time - the more conventional set up was one or two units at the stern - but *Jupiter* and her sister ships had the propulsion units fitted at both ends, both fore and aft along a central axis. I never discovered why this had happened, but clearly even the experts from Voith that I met were surprised when they came to give me my induction briefing. They had no practical experience of such a complex set up and the reality was that I had to experiment on my own quite a bit to establish exactly how best to handle the ship. Looking back, I have to say that once you mastered the complexity of the Voith system, it was a joy to use.

It was great working with the Voith people and a nice surprise that their key representative was Arthur Naismith, a talented New Zealander I had first met on my very first voyage on the *Hollypark* as a young apprentice. We had hit it off right away

on that initial two-year posting, and had kept in touch ever since. Arthur was a great friend, and for many years sent me a whole New Zealand lamb at Christmas. Each December a refrigerated van would come up from the docks to our house in Greenock to drop off a frozen carcass all wrapped up in muslin, as though delivering to the local butcher. In those days we didn't have a fridge, so my poor wife Ann had to store it in the bath while she made hurried arrangements to have it properly cut up and shared with family and friends.

Taking on the pioneering role as the first Captain to use the Voith system, however, also meant that I in turn effectively became CalMac's own unofficial Voith training officer. This meant I spent many more hours at the helm than would be normal, helping colleagues get to grips with the complexities of controlling the two opposing thrust units that supplied both propulsion and steering.

Over the next 35 years the *Jupiter* gave long and varied service, principally on the Gourock-Dunoon route, but also on the Wemyss Bay-Rothesay and Ardrossan-Brodick runs. I used to enjoy bringing her to Gourock pier as, unlike most vessels, you could bring her alongside ready to meet the linkspan at the stern, in an almost continuous single running sweep - if you lined her up correctly. She was a worthy workhorse, but also came with quite a bit of passenger accommodation and proper teak decking. Though far from luxurious compared to ships like the *Queen Mary II*, or the *Jeanie Deans*, she also did a fair amount of special excursions and summer cruising in her day.

Jupiter mid-run (Bryan Kennedy)

Lamont's launch lunch for *Jupiter* November 1973 -
Turkey and Christmas pudding all round!

FACT SHEET

- Built: 1973, Lamont, Port Glasgow
- Entered service: 1974
- Left service: 2010
- Length: 218 ft
- Tonnage: 849 tons
- Speed: 13 kts
- Capacity: 687 passengers, 40 cars
- Vehicle handling: side and rear loading via linkspans

VIEW FROM THE BRIDGE

Wemyss Bay-Rothesay was probably the easier of the main postings with its slightly shorter evening hours. Rothesay, however, also meant three or four nights away from home as the boats lay there overnight where it was much less exposed than Wemyss Bay. Lying there also meant we were ready for the 06.25 sailing that connected with the early 'Businessman's Train' to Glasgow - in those days we had quite a few regular commuters to take across as Bute has always been a desirable place to live.

The Rothesay run had an interesting and varied clientele - from the Marquis of Bute, who could always be relied upon each year after one of his shoots to bring a beautiful brace of pheasants to the bridge, to Lord Attenborough and his family and friends going up to the estate at Rhubodach. Once, even Madonna made her way across en-route to Stella McCartney's wedding at Mount Stuart - although I'm not sure what she made of the Station Bar at Wemyss Bay as she ducked in to escape the paparazzi while waiting for the boat.

The Bute Highland Games was a highlight each year - especially the parade back to the pier at the end of the day. But perhaps the most memorable sporting event on the island was the arrival of F1 in 2003, when the current Marquis hosted a celebration of motor racing on his estate in the Mount Stuart Classic. In his earlier years, he had been a successful competitor and a Le Mans 24-hour race winner, driving less formally as Johnny Dumfries. It must have been a poignant moment to hear the scream of an F1 engine on his estate's narrow tree-lined roads. The old Victorian resort hotels in Rothesay and Dunoon also had a fair smattering of VIPs as visitors,

not least when hosting party conferences, but probably the less said about them the better. It nearly always ended up with them briefly visiting us on the bridge and making small talk about the weather, the state of the piers or the number of cars we were taking across - even as the cost of petrol soared. I do remember once on the Dunoon run, ending up with the local Sheriff on the bridge. He lived in Greenock and commuted, so he was a frequent traveller that we knew well enough. This particular day, he was sitting in the passenger lounge on his way home when he suddenly realised that three of his fellow passengers were men he had, just an hour or so earlier, found guilty of a serious Breach of the Peace and fined them £100 each. We agreed that on this occasion, a visit to the Bridge for the full duration of the sail might be a sensible plan.

The Gourock-Dunoon rosters were the harder, but at least I got home every night. That said, with a first sailing of the day at 06.45 it meant leaving home at 04.45 – not the happiest of prospects on a dark January morning with the wind howling and the rain lashing down, and the rest of the family snug and warm in their beds. Typical days consisted of 17-hour shifts, and with a requirement to do the crossing in 20 minutes, with a 10-minute turn around, it meant two dockings and departures every hour: fifteen double runs a day. Shifts normally went six days on, one day off. One lesser-known occupational hazard was the regular cup of coffee clocked up each and every trip - the kettle up on the bridge went on immediately after leaving the pier, but at thirty trips a day it proved too much for most of us and more than one Captain must have had caffeine poisoning!

Much of the time Dunoon was dominated by the US Navy facility in the Holy Loch with its massive dry dock and support vessels for their Polaris Fleet. For just over thirty years countless thousands of US servicemen and their families crossed and re-crossed on the ferries. They provided some excitement to the area and quite a boost to the local economy - not for nothing was Dunoon once known to have the greatest number of taxis per head of population in the western world.

Dunoon was of course also famous for the Cowal Games in the last weekend of August, one of the high spots of the Highland Games Season. The Games were also an eventful time for us: extra sailings, pipe-bands holding impromptu rehearsals on the open car deck and athletes, caber throwers, highland dancers in traditional attire and spectators all crowding on board together. The boats were packed to the gunnels - 500-600 people per crossing for much of Friday and Saturday. The last sailing back to Gourock on a games weekend was a nightmare, with people desperately running up the pier moments before we sailed and a lot of passengers much the worse for wear.

One time, we had a massive US sailor on board, 6ft 6in and 16 stone of him, and off his head on something or other. He was convinced he was Jesus, so naturally enough decided that he would just walk on water for the final hundred metres or so between boat and pier. We had a terrible time trying to pull him back on board when he discovered he wasn't who he thought he was.

My most memorable trip on the Gourock-Dunoon run, however, was actually on the *Maid of Cumbrae* some years before the *Jupiter* took over.

We were sailing in dense fog using radar. Normally there would be very little else moving around on the Clyde in these conditions, and if there were, it would certainly be with extreme caution. Eric Harkness, the Mate, suddenly detected an object on the screen moving at speed and seemingly on a collision course. We made to starboard to give her room, but she seemed to change course too. We weren't sure what it was but it was clear it was moving at about 20 knots - suicidal in these conditions! We changed course again, and again she did the same. The only option left was to stop…and wait…and hope. Eric and I were convinced we were doomed. Just at the moment we were anticipating an imminent impact, there was an almighty whoosh, a very loud sound of revving engines being slammed into reverse and a great surge of churning water. Out of the dense bank of fog came a sixty-foot long, grey and black US Navy fast-response tender. It juddered to a halt beside us, engines still throbbing, and a loud Yankee voice boomed out:

'Hey man, can you give us a course to the aircraft carrier?'

Very relieved we obliged and, after waving goodbye, went off to check our underwear. The boat was evidently off the 30,000 ton Essex Class aircraft carrier USS *Wasp*, that was on a short, week-long goodwill visit to the Clyde - the *Wasp* had fought in the Pacific in World War II, and had played an important part in the American space programme. It was the recovery ship for five of the Gemini missions that led to the Apollo Moon-shot programme, including Buzz Aldrin's first flight in space in Gemini XII.

It seemed the crew were trying to get back to the carrier, which because of its immense size, had to lie in deep water and was anchored in mid-river off the Tail of the Bank. Small

Jupiter battles her way across to Dunoon in February 1982   rivals in the background (Greenock Telegraph)

boats were constantly ferrying crew and visitors back and forward to shore and to its escort vessels anchored nearby. The tender didn't have radar and, when the fog came in, had found itself hopelessly lost. It seems, however, that they had managed to pick up the sound of our engines in the stillness of the fog and had homed in on us as their only hope of finding a route back before they ran aground. All perfectly reasonable, but why on earth they were doing so at 20 knots, in absolute-zero visibility and without ever once sounding a horn or whistle, is still beyond me.

SHIP'S LOG

The Gourock-Dunoon service was a valued, profitable service for CalMac. When the Streakers arrived in 1974, CalMac was already carrying over one million passengers and 150,000 cars and commercial vehicles a year on the route. Over latter years, however, it suffered a 'death of a thousand cuts', as arguments raged over competition policy, potential cross subsidies and the niceties of EU tendering procedures. Gradually this meant the service was stripped back to one sailing an hour and, eventually, withdrawn altogether. I have mixed emotions about my time on the *Jupiter*. Newer innovations and better passenger accommodation were brought in to CalMac over time on a great number of routes, outshining the Streakers in many respects, but we had nonetheless worked the Dunoon service up to become a flagship service - so it was doubly sad to see it wither away in the latter years.

By 2006, the *Jupiter* had become the oldest and longest-serving vessel in the fleet but she could not remain in service forever, and in 2011 the old girl was eventually sold for breaking up after thirty-six years.

The Old Man of the Sea at the Voith Schneider controls, *Jupiter* (Keith Goss, courtesy of Ships Monthly)

Jeanie Deans at Craigendoran July 1964 - Culture and Sport Glasgow (Glasgow Museums)

BUILT FOR SUMMER CRUISING WHEN CLYDE CRUISING WAS AT ITS ZENITH, THE JEANIE DEANS WAS ONE OF A NUMBER OF ELEGANT PADDLE STEAMERS WORKING OUT OF CRAIGENDORAN. SHE MAINLY DID THE FLAGSHIP LOCHGOILHEAD/ARROCHAR CRUISES, AND WAS UNDOUBTEDLY ONE OF THE MOST MAGNIFICENT BOATS ON THE CLYDE FOR THE BEST PART OF THIRTY YEARS.

The *Jeanie Deans* on a perfect summer's day (CRSC)

FACT SHEET

- Built: 1931, Fairfields, Govan
- Entered service: 1931
- Left service: 1964
- Length: 250 ft
- Tonnage: 635 tons
- Speed: 14 kts
- Capacity: 1,400 passengers

VIEW FROM THE BRIDGE

Fast, graceful and well appointed, it was sad that she was taken out of service in the mid-sixties, when modernism was king and few people appreciated the real value of preserving the best of the past. I can remember her with 1200 aboard, churning through the river full-steam ahead on glorious summer evenings in deep blue water, glistening in the sun. If people want to wax lyrical about the heyday of Clyde Cruising, then they must surely mention the *Jeanie Deans*.

We didn't always sail in sunny weather, of course, but we had to keep services running regardless. Fog was the real problem. In the days before we had reliable radar (only introduced on the paddle steamers in the early sixties), we had to draw on our own years of experience, backed up by meticulous practice. A cold front settling over the Clyde could cause the most horrendous dense fogs for days on end. The sort of fog I'm talking about thankfully no longer occurs, but back in the early sixties, Greenock and Gourock still had heavy industry, not to mention thousands of homes all heated by coal fires and all belching smoke into the air. That's bad enough, but add to that the thousands of extra tons of soot and smoke drifting down from Glasgow, and you have a truly toxic cocktail. The smoke and soot mixed with the fog and the resulting smog made it impossible to see more than a few yards ahead. When it rolled in, it was likely to stay for days, sometimes weeks.

We had to continue to offer a lifeline service to the Clyde ports despite the fog and we did so by 'dead reckoning': not much heard of now in these days of GPS and other digital navigation devices. We would run predetermined bearings, at an exact speed (42 revs per minute in the case of a paddle steamer) and for a precise time measured in seconds. At the right moment the helmsman would turn on to the new course, repeating the pattern over and over until we neared the pier. Over the last few hundred yards we were guided in solely by the sound of a pier-hand blowing regularly on a whistle, all the while listening out for a fog-horn from any other vessel brave enough to venture out.

We practised setting the courses we would use in the fog on clear days so that, on the days when we had poor visibility, we could repeat the manoeuvres exactly. We knew the tides and we could assume minimal wind when fog hung in the air. In all the years that we did this we never, ever, had a problem but this was because, at least once a week, with conditions just right, we would rehearse and rehearse, checking timings with stopwatches. Talk about a wing and a prayer? Gone are the days…

Food was a key element of daily life on all ships. The crew worked long hours and they had to be adequately fuelled. In the days of the *Jeanie Deans* meals were served formally, at least to the officers and their guests: three-course meals, silver service, china teapots and emblemed plates and crockery, all on starched white tablecloths, and served by immaculately uniformed stewards - none of your Assistant Tea Room Attendants (ATRAs) in nylon overalls in those days. Meal times worked in with the demands of the timetables, early starts and late finishes, and as a consequence we tended to eat early, with breakfast at 6am, lunch at 11am and high tea (or dinner) from 4.30pm in the afternoon. This is one thing I lived with for many, many years - and in some ways, still do - to this day, come five o'clock, I am always ready for a proper meal.

We didn't just look after the crew of course, we were ever mindful of the need to attend to our passengers. We once took a consignment of over 1,000 homing pigeons to Bute. In the fifties and sixties, pigeon-racing clubs across the country would often send their pigeons, unaccompanied, to starting destinations up to sixty miles away by rail (and also in this case by boat). Released at a predetermined time the pigeons would fly back to their home lofts, their arrival time carefully recorded on special clocks, and their average speeds calculated to determine an overall winner.

This particular day the wicker baskets containing the individual pigeon cages were all carefully stacked on a trolley on the main deck. All we were required to do was to deliver them and to ensure that they had adequate water on the journey out. Mid-voyage, one of the catering staff went to check on the birds. He was quite an animal lover and took pity on them all cooped up.

On the bridge - note the wooden 'dodgers' folded down in the background - our only protection against the gales

Silver sauce boat detail from the *Jeanie Deans* - she was originally part of the London and North Eastern Railway fleet.

He decided that as well as providing water he should let them enjoy a wee bit more fresh air and a chance to exercise their legs, and so he opened up all the cages. After a few tentative peeks out the cage doors there was suddenly a loud beating of wings and 999 pigeons rushed into the sky… One solitary pigeon remained and duly took some water. We never did hear if they all got back.

SHIP'S LOG

The *Jeanie Deans* was withdrawn in 1964 after thirty years on the Clyde. She lay idle for a year until, in late 1965, she became *Queen of the South* for a short while, having been sold to run on what was to become an ill-fated venture cruising on the Thames - where she had, in fact, been many years before as a wartime minesweeper and anti-aircraft ship, the HMS *Jeanie Deans*, Penant No J108. At the end of her second season on the Thames she was sold to a Belgian breakers yard. A sad end to a fine ship with a great heritage.

HMS *Jeanie Deans* at war © Imperial War Museum (HU 100146)

SEVEN PS WAVERLEY

Waverley approaching Ayr Harbour (Bryan Kennedy)

SURELY THE WAVERLEY IS THE ICONIC CLYDE STEAMER? WHY RATE HER ONLY SEVENTH AND AFTER THE JEANIE DEANS? WELL, SHE MAY WELL BE THE BEST-KNOWN REPRESENTATIVE OF A LONG-GONE ERA, BUT I'M AFRAID SHE WAS SIMPLY NOT THE BEST. SHE IS, HOWEVER, A TRUE SURVIVOR AND IN THE COLD COMMERCIAL WORLD OF TODAY THAT IS QUITE AN ACHIEVEMENT AND FULLY DESERVING OF A SPECIAL MENTION.

Austere times, the launch of the *Waverley* in October 1946 - Culture and Sport Glasgow (Glasgow Museums)

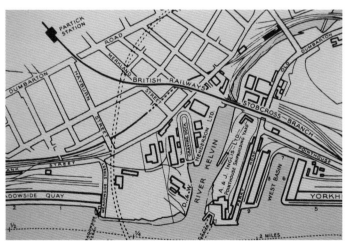

Detail from November 1960 Clyde Navigation Trust Map showing the mouth of the River Kelvin and A&J Inglis Shipyard where the *Waverley* was built and launched (above). The Riverside Museum, Scotland's Museum of Travel and Transport and European Museum of the Year 2013, is now on the site.

Nearly scrapped, nearly sunk and nearly floating off as museum piece, she has confounded them all and grown to win a special place in so many hearts. And yes, she has also become a fully working reminder of the glory days of Clyde Cruising. But from the outset she was always a victim of her humble 'post-war austerity' start in life. Built in 1946/47 with war compensation money to replace her namesake (sunk by enemy action at Dunkirk in 1940), she was made of low-quality steel plate, much of it recycled from ships being scrapped.

Consequently, throughout the time I sailed on her, she had a considerable battle with rust. Her internal fit-out was rather basic and over the years she also suffered a bit of general neglect and so, in all honesty, I can't really think of her as having the kudos of the pre-war paddlers. She never really had the following of the *Caledonia* or the *Queen Mary II*. Her following was to come later.

Far from refined, she was very utilitarian, and not a patch on, say, the *Jeanie Deans*. As for her handling, I called her 'the sledge'; she had a tiny rudder so that you had to give her an enormous amount of room to turn. Going into Rothesay for instance, you had to go hard over as you passed the Glenburn Hotel just to get on to the pier - and that's nearly a mile out.

One thing that rarely gets a mention in talking about the *Waverley* as a working boat is its role in servicing the liners that regularly called in at Greenock as part of the regular transatlantic route to Canada and New York. The *Waverley*, *Caledonia* and *The Maids* all served as tenders, taking passengers from Princes Pier to liners such as the Canadian Pacific's *Empress of Scotland* (pictured opposite) and Cunard's *Carinthia*. This was actually quite a tricky manoeuvre, especially in a paddle steamer and quite a test of seamanship. These big liners were swaying around their anchor with the water breaking off the bow. The paddle steamers didn't have quick responses, and you needed to plan carefully to work out how the ship was swinging, and how best to approach. It was not uncommon to transfer up to 400 people and luggage at a time often in choppy conditions. As late as 1961, some 120 transatlantic crossings called in at Greenock: quite an international route-centre in its day. You could pick up a boat going to Largs, Dunoon, Craigendoran, Ayr, Millport, Rothesay, Montreal, Quebec or even New York.

Waverley as tender to Canadian Pacific transatlantic liner *Empress of Scotland* off the Tail of the Bank 1954 (Bruce Peter/Dr Ann Glen Collection)

CHAPTER SEVEN: PS WAVERLEY

Waverley in CalMac livery – red funnels with lion emblem (CRSC)

Waverley at Innellan CSPC colours, Summer 1968 - Culture and Sport Glasgow (Glasgow Museums)

- Paddle steamer
- Built: 1947, A & J Inglis, Glasgow
- Entered service: 1947
- Left CalMac service: 1973
- Length: 240 ft
- Tonnage: 693 tons
- Speed: 14 kts
- Capacity: 1,350 passengers

VIEW FROM THE BRIDGE

I worked on her, off and on, as either Master or Mate for four summer seasons in the early sixties. But I suppose my main memory of her was a day in high summer in 1977 (15th July to be precise), when she was no longer a CalMac ship and I was taking the *Jupiter* over to Dunoon on its regular hourly ferry crossing.

The *Waverley* was some distance off to the south-west, also heading to Dunoon. The pier is big enough to accommodate both vessels and so I was not too concerned about who might be arriving first. But rather than get there before us the *Waverley* unfortunately ended up on top of the Gantocks - a notorious, but well charted and well marked rocky reef a couple of miles off shore. A ship on the rocks: not a sight any of us ever wanted to see.

I was ready to provide assistance if needed but, as it turned out, the USS *Hunley* (the US Polaris Submarine Tender that in those days was stationed nearby in the Holy Loch) was much better equipped for rescue work, and she was rapidly able to send over tenders, pumps and rescue crews. I'm pleased to say all aboard escaped unhurt.

The *Waverley* herself was quite badly damaged and was lucky to survive. As the tide went out she could easily have broken her back, effectively writing her off for good. It seems likely she only survived because of her post war design. Despite the poor quality of some materials, her design had been based around the possible need for her to be called into active service as a minesweeper, just like her ill-fated predecessor, in any fresh conflict. In those days the Admiralty regularly reviewed all UK merchant-ship construction plans and could order (and also pay for) alterations and additions they thought might be useful in the event she had to be requisitioned. The *Waverley* had been significantly strengthened to cope with the possible addition of a gun turret on the foredeck (including permanent fittings that were hidden under her wooden decking) and the fixings and support structure necessary to attach minesweeping gear aft.

I also tend to think that, ultimately, the dramatic situation in which she found herself that day might have actually helped in her longer-term preservation. Not only did it make the headlines, but it also dramatically brought into sharp focus that she was very nearly lost - the last of her kind. People suddenly saw her as something that was well worth saving. And so, despite my earlier disparaging comments, she really was a special ship in her own way, a real survivor.

Strangely enough she wasn't the only ship to hit trouble on the Gantocks that year - only 4 months later, the ML *Fulgor* (the Clyde Port Authority's lighthouse tender vessel) ran aground while trying to service the Gantock light, and I ended up having to go to her assistance, pulling her clear before she was tipped over on the receding tide. We managed to get a line on board fairly quickly, but I do remember one of my officers excitedly launching distress flares that, interestingly enough, garnered absolutely no response whatsoever from any other vessel on the Clyde. About a week later, I received a very nice letter of thanks from the CPA enclosing a cheque - it just about covered the cost of a round of drinks for the crew.

My last involvement with the *Waverley* was actually one gusty day in April 1997, eighteen months after I left CalMac. I had

Waverley going astern at berth in Ayr (Bryan Kennedy)

Awaiting orders in the *Waverley* engine room - Paddle Steamer Preservation Society Cruise October 2013

Waverley (in her original LNER colours) packed to the gunnels cruising on the Thames, September 2013 (R Dikstra)

been asked to stand in as Master at very short notice to take charge of a full-day cruise out to Campbeltown via Helensburgh, Largs and several other ports. It must have been over 20 years since I had last been on her, but it was nice to see some familiar faces and I am glad to say that the trip went exactly to plan - and later I was able to sit back and think I had played at least a small part in its new life, whilst enjoying the bottle of whisky they kindly sent me in recognition of my services that day.

SHIP'S LOG

Bought from CalMac for £1 in 1973 by the Paddle Steamer Preservation Society, the *Waverley* has now spent considerably more years in service with them than she ever did with CalMac or its commercial predecessors. She underwent a major lottery-funded refit between 2001-03 and continues to cruise the Summer Season on the Clyde in addition to fitting in short visits to the Bristol Channel and the Thames – rightly allowing her to continue to promote herself as the 'Last Sea-Going Paddle Steamer in the World'.

EIGHT DEPV TALISMAN

Talisman at Rothesay 1963 - Culture and Sport Glasgow (Glasgow Museums)

BUILT A FEW YEARS BEFORE WORLD WAR II, TALISMAN WAS AHEAD OF HER TIME – A DIESEL ELECTRIC PADDLE VESSEL – THE ONLY ONE OF ITS KIND AND A REAL WORLD FIRST. HOWEVER, AS WITH MANY TRAILBLAZERS SHE HAD PROBLEMS. SHE SUFFERED SIGNIFICANT RELIABILITY PROBLEMS IN HER PRE-WAR DAYS AND IT SEEMS SHE WAS DESTINED TO BE DISPOSED OF, OR MORE LIKELY, SCRAPPED ALTOGETHER.

The *Talisman* approaching Wemyss Bay pier (CRSC)

The war actually saved her as, like many others on the Clyde, she was requisitioned by the Admiralty and managed to complete her war service competently enough as HMS *Aristocrat*. She even had a small walk-on part at the Normandy landings. Again, in the shortages and austerity of a post-war world, she managed to soldier on regardless. Eventually, in 1954 she was refitted with new engines and thereafter her fortunes changed. By the time I joined her, she was regarded as both reliable and highly efficient, using only 0.6 tons of diesel per hour at an 'economical' cruising speed of 14 knots.

FACT SHEET

- Built: 1935, A & J Inglis, Pointhouse, Glasgow
- Entered service: 1935
- Left service: 1966
- Length: 215 ft
- Tonnage: 544 tons
- Speed: 17 kts
- Capacity: 1,252 passengers

VIEW FROM THE BRIDGE

The first summer season I worked on her, the *Talisman* would lie over at Millport every night. Naively, I thought if we hired a wee cottage there during the holidays, then I would be able to see the family every evening. I soon found out, however, that summer cruising schedules didn't quite work like that. Two days after the family arrived, I was suddenly posted to Craigendoran - in the days before the Erskine Bridge, this was probably about as far away as you could possibly get. This meant that I didn't see the family for the entire month apart from my one day off each week - as far as I was concerned, they might as well have stayed at home and, even now, years later my son and daughter, Glenn and Kay still remember being told to 'wave to daddy' as my boat sailed past on our way to Ayr.

I liked the *Talisman* - I only knew her as a re-engined ship, of course, first joining her in 1959, but to me she was quite responsive, had a fair turn of speed if needed and had that unmistakable, quietly efficient, hum. Although she was truly a world first, I was more than interested to see the new public body responsible for the CalMac fleet and infrastructure (Caledonian

Marine Assets Ltd (CMAL)) recently promoting their new 'low-emission hybrid ferry' MV *Hallaig* as a ground-breaker. It's great to see such innovation still on the Clyde, but of course the *Talisman* 'diesel-electric paddle vessel' was the precursor and a ground-breaker herself. As my mother always said: 'There's nothing new under the sun'.

Funnily enough, the *Hallaig* was built in Ferguson's at Port Glasgow for the Skye to Raasay service. The Western Isles supplied many a CalMac crewman to the Clyde. One long-time captain of the *Talisman* was Colin John McKay. I remember him in his lilting tones explaining an incident at Wemyss Bay one winter's evening to an informal committee of enquiry:

'We were on our final approach to the pier…when su-dden-lee there was…a flash of dark-en-ness and there we were up-on the shore'

I was on the *Bute* that night, tied up on the opposite side of the pier at Wemyss Bay and saw the incident Captain McKay was referring to, but even I took a few seconds to work out exactly what he meant. That night there had been a power cut at the crucial moment of his final approach to the pier. Every light on the pier and onshore had suddenly gone out. He could see nothing, but he was already committed to docking. It was impossible for him to judge exactly where he was in those vital few minutes as he came alongside the pier so I suppose, in that wonderful Highland way of his, he was right: it was a 'flash of dark-en-ness'. Only a Teuchter could describe a power cut in such a poetic way.

Wemyss Bay is a railhead pier built to serve Rothesay but the station itself also served the coastal communities of Skelmorlie and Wemyss Bay. In late Victorian and Edwardian times, these

Talisman docked at Wemyss Bay Pier, Summer 1965, *Queen Mary II* in the background (CRSC)

Wemyss Bay Station floral displays (Rev H.D.E. Rokeby Collection, Royal Commission of Ancient & Historical Monuments of Scotland)

communities were akin to Glasgow's version of New York's 'The Hamptons' of Great Gatsby fame. Magnificent red sandstone mansions designed to impress were built along the shoreline and cliff edge to be used for weekend entertaining in the summer season by the West of Scotland's wealthy industrial elite. All summer the waters immediately off shore were filled with large private steam yachts and racers. Not for nothing was the Clyde home to one of the world's finest yacht builders: Fife's of Fairlie. Fife yachts are now highly valued and regarded as classics of their time. William Fife also designed two America's Cup Challengers for Sir Thomas Lipton – Shamrock I & III.

Weymss Bay station itself was rebuilt in 1903 to better serve this affluent client base and its 'Chinese Tudor' exterior, sweeping glass interior and unique sloping covered promenade to link with the pier-side make it a gem of Edwardian railway architecture. The station also gained an enviable reputation as one of the most beautiful in Scotland. People would wax lyrical about its stunning year-round displays of hanging baskets and its colourful overflowing flower planters.

To us on the boats, however, it all meant something rather different. We saw docking at Wemyss Bay as a constant problem: the staff were so busy watering their baskets and tending their plants that there was never anyone about to catch the bl**dy ropes!

SHIP'S LOG

The *Talisman* only ventured out of the Clyde during her war service years as HMS *Aristocrat*. She was withdrawn in 1966, and despite being put up for sale, she was eventually broken up at Dalmuir on the north side of the river in 1967.

A busy Wemyss Bay Station in the early days (Watt Library, Inverclyde Council)

The *Glen Sannox*, March 1974 (CRSC)

A CLASSIC SIDE-LOADING CAR FERRY OF THE LATE 1950'S. THE GLEN SANNOX WAS A RESPONSIVE SHIP – AS LONG AS SHE WAS MOVING SHE WAS STEERING – SOUNDS OBVIOUS BUT ACTUALLY I HAVE TO SAY IT'S NOT VERY COMMON, AND UNLIKE MOST SHIPS, SHE WAS STILL RESPONSIVE RIGHT UP TO THE MOMENT WE ACTUALLY STOPPED.

Proving her versatility, the *Glen Sannox* here in her cruising role,
CalMac poster Summer 1979

FACT SHEET

- Built: 1957, Ailsa Shipyard, Troon
- Entered service: 1957
- Left service: 1989
- Length: 244ft
- Tonnage: 1,269 tons
- Speed: 16 kts
- Capacity: 1100 passengers, 55 cars
- Vehicle handling: originally side ramps but stern ramp fitted later

VIEW FROM THE BRIDGE

I was on the *Sannox* frequently, mainly on the Arran run but I mention her here as she really helps to illustrate the variety of life as Ship's Master in CalMac at the time. The *Glen Sannox* was built specifically for the Arran route: basically an enlarged version of the ABC's. A well-loved boat with clean lines, she could take up to 50 cars. When she first entered service, some questioned the need for such a large car-carrying capacity but such was the demand, the *Glen Sannox* also soon had to increase the frequency of the service to four return trips a day.

With services criss-crossing the Clyde for up to 364 days a year, it was inevitable that someone, somewhere would be thinking of ways to 'work the system'. The routes with fast turnarounds were particularly prone to problems, as the emphasis was on getting people on and off the ship rather than the detailed checking of every ticket against every passenger. Stories of 'discount' tickets being available in such-and-such a bar were frequent. There was also a tendency to feel that friends and family could be treated to the occasional freebie. The Company therefore had a constant battle to protect its revenue. By tradition, tickets were only sold on-board at the Purser's Office. As Captain, I had an overall responsibility for everything that happened on the ship, but my prime duty was always in ensuring the safety of the ship and passengers. A safe docking and passage was always the priority. On routes with a 10-minute turnaround, that usually didn't leave much time for anything else. However, when I did get an opportunity to supervise what was actually happening at the gangways I often found there had been a last-minute, inexplicable surge in demand for tickets!

Stories of scams and schemes that were uncovered were many, but my favourite was told to me by one of the office staff at Gourock. They had noticed an ongoing discrepancy with passenger and vehicle numbers on one of the wee ferries linking the smaller islands up North. The passenger tickets simply did not tally with the number of cars being transported. In seeking an explanation, they were blithely told,

'Well, now, that'll be the change in the type of vehicles we're getting on the crossing nowadays - you see, we're getting an awful lot of these new 'au-to-ma-tic cars'.

There's no answer to an explanation like that...

In the early seventies as traffic further increased, the *Sannox* was replaced by the *Caledonia*, CalMac's first roll-on, roll-off ferry on the Clyde. The *Sannox* was then used for relief work and specifically to ferry workers to the Ardyne Oil Platform Fabrication Yard (one of many such yards that appeared in unlikely remote locations around the Scottish coast as a result of the early seventies North Sea Oil Boom). Ardyne is a relatively isolated spot on the Cowal Peninsula immediately opposite Rothesay. There, over a four or five year period, the engineering giant Sir Robert McAlpine built three massive oil platforms for Shell, including the 300,000 ton Cormorant A platform. When it was completed, Cormorant A was the biggest such structure in the world at 100m square (total area 10,000 square metres) and 172m high.

Every day, seven days a week, we took hundreds of workers from Wemyss Bay to the yard's own purpose-built pier. This was a special passenger service supplementing the nearby Gourock-Dunoon car ferry.

Glen Sannox off Gourock, August 1977 (CRSC)

The 300,000 ton Cormorant A nears completion - image courtesy
Sir Robert McAlpine

Glen Sannox leaving Rothesay (Anthony Williams)

We referred to the men, rather dismissively, as Bog Arabs, but these were tough men, doing tough demanding work. I was always amused, however to see that the woman in charge of the bar – 'Big May' - ruled them with a rod of iron. Unbelievably, looking back on it now, the bar on board the *Glen Sannox* was open first thing in the morning for these guys as they went off to their work, not just at the end of their working day. It's amazing to think in these days of strict health and safety procedures that a ship, taking people to work on heavy plant and machinery, and at heights up to 400ft, should be happily selling them alcohol at eight o'clock in the morning, but there you are: different times. If one of the men so much as spilled a drop of beer on Big May's nice shiny lino, however, they would have a mop thrust at them and told to 'clean the *!#**#!* mess up….NOW!' And, believe me, they always did.

Despite its massive scale, the Ardyne Yard was short-lived. It has, however, left its mark. The two giant tidal basins that were gouged out to accommodate platform construction are still clearly visible even today. They have permanently changed the coast-line on the southern tip of Cowal.

In mid-1977 I also took the *Glen Sannox* round the top of Scotland to the Hall Russell Shipyard in Aberdeen for a major refit and new engines in preparation for a changed role or possible sale. Overhauls on this scale are unusual, and involve considerable planning and supervision from owners and yard staff alike. In this case, myself, our First Officer, the Chief Engineer and three of his team were all there on site for many months, ensuring everything was done exactly as it should be. Engineers in particular like to be involved early, as it helps their understanding of every last detail of the workings of the new engines.

After the refit we went out on trials in Aberdeen Bay. The weather wasn't good when we set out but it steadily worsened as the afternoon progressed and the ship started to roll quite a bit. In all my years I never suffered from sea sickness, but the same can't be said for the staff of the Maritime and Coastguard Agency (MCA) who were there to supervise the trials. The shipyard employees weren't too happy either, with a few looking more than a bit 'green about the gills'. The weather continued to worsen with the waves tossing us about and, at one point, the Engineering Superintendent was sent flying right across the wheelhouse. Although he was uninjured, that was enough for most of them and they all wanted to get back to the safety of the harbour ASAP. Unfortunately the pilot then told me there were a number of oil rig supply vessels

Glen Sannox sets off on a calm morning - Culture and Sport Glasgow (Glasgow Museums)

already waiting ahead of us in a queue and we'd have to wait our turn. Only after another half hour was I finally able to take her in.

Once back safe and snug in the harbour, the MCA people had to pick up their briefcases and coats which they had left in the purser's office during the trip. That was supposed to be the 'secure' part of the ship where items such as fire extinguishers were stored during the refit work. When they opened the door they discovered an office full of foam. One of the more violent rolls had set off the extinguishers and it was like a lucky dip as they felt their way about in the foam looking for their belongings. It seems the majority of vessels using Aberdeen had considerably deeper draughts than the *Glen Sannox*!

It turned out that the new engines were considerably lighter than the originals. The full effect of this on her handling only became apparent on my return to Gourock. She very nearly didn't stop at the pier. She promptly had to be fitted with additional ballast tanks to get her to settle back to her original marks.

All in all, it was an interesting few months in a role that few Masters these days get to experience.

SHIP'S LOG

The *Glen Sannox* ended her days as the Al Basmallah taking pilgrims to Jeddah and was finally scrapped after running aground. The hot sun of the Red Sea must have been quite a wake-up call after being so long on the West Coast of Scotland.

Glen Sannox berthing alongside the *Juno* at Dunoon Summer 1978 (Michael Magnay)

TEN MV CALEDONIAN ISLES

Caledonian Isles off Brodick, spring morning in March (Bryan Kennedy)

THE LAST LARGE 5,000+ TON SHIP I COMMANDED – SHE REPLACED THE 3,000 TON ISLE OF ARRAN WHICH I HAD ALSO HELPED GET UP AND RUNNING ON THE ARDROSSAN-BRODICK RUN. THE ISLE OF ARRAN WAS ONLY ABOUT TEN YEARS OLD WHEN SHE WAS REPLACED BY THE CALEDONIAN ISLES AND MOVED UP NORTH TO KENNACRAIG AND ISLAY, BUT THE FACT IS THAT, ALMOST FROM THE OUTSET, SHE HAD STRUGGLED TO KEEP UP WITH THE RAPID GROWTH IN VEHICLE TRAFFIC TO THE TOURIST MAGNET THAT IS ARRAN.

Caledonian Isles on launch day Lowestoft May 25th 1993 (courtesy of Eastern Daily Press)

The Arran route seems to be proof of the phrase 'build it and they will come', as come they did: in their droves. People, it seems, just cannot get enough of the island they call 'Scotland in Miniature', but who could blame them? It's a very beautiful island with an incredible range of geology, and one that offers a nice relaxed pace of life. The *Caledonian Isles* herself offered very comfortable passenger space and I certainly enjoyed sailing her, although the constant overnight layovers, even at somewhere as picturesque as Brodick, do lose their charm after a while.

FACT SHEET

- Built: 1993, Richards, Lowestoft
- Entered service: 1993
- Left service: continuing
- Length: 310 ft
- Tonnage: 5220 tons
- Speed: 15kts
- Capacity: 1000 passengers, 110 cars (with mezzanine)
- Vehicle handling: roll-on, roll-off

VIEW FROM THE BRIDGE

The ship had generous passenger accommodation giving people plenty of options for the one-hour scheduled sail from Ardrossan (or the two-hour diversion to Gourock in bad weather). Bad-weather diversions are a nightmare for everyone, but sometimes there is just no alternative and the Arran route, I have to concede, has more than its fair share. The micro-climate in the waters between Ardrossan and Arran has a significant influence on the surrounding weather patterns and over the years has been an important area of interest for the Met Office. The *Caledonian Isles*, like its predecessors before it, was therefore equipped with a full weather station.

One of the Captain's responsibilities was to ensure we took readings every four hours and sent the records off to the Met Office. Over the years we received considerable thanks for our dedication in attending to the observations and in helping improve weather forecasting for the area.

The worst sailing I ever experienced on the Clyde was from Arran. It was on the predecessor to the Caledonian Isles, the *Isle of Arran*. We had 20ft waves and the weather was so bad I knew we couldn't get her into Ardrossan and I had no option but to steam up and down the Firth in the hope of riding out the storm: even the more sheltered Gourock to the North was too much of a challenge that day. Three hours later things subsided and we were finally able to get in, get unloaded and begin the clear up.

The problem at Ardrossan is not just that the harbour is quite exposed, but depth is also a real issue, as it changes so rapidly on the approach. On the way into Adrossan, quite close to the harbour entrance, you suddenly cross from the very deep water of the Firth to quite shallow water. The consequence of this is that as you approach, the swell picks up viciously. If, on top of that, you're beam on to the weather (wind at 90 degrees to the direction of travel), and given the large sea area to 'gather it up', then you find the ship is constantly being knocked off course. To maintain direction you therefore need to maintain strong forward momentum, but as soon as you are in the harbour you only have a relatively small area in which to slow a 5,000 ton vessel, make the sharp turn and berth the ship. There is therefore a limit to what is possible and sometimes diversion is the only option. To some extent you also just have to have faith in the bow thrust coming up to power when required.

Even when you are inside the harbour, the problems don't go away. The swell can still be extreme and on more than one occasion I've had to abort an attempt to unload as the ship rolled around at its berth. Imagine the frustration all round when people are so close to getting ashore and we have to sail back out and divert to Gourock, a good hour away. So, all in all, I always felt a certain pride in getting the *Caledonian Isles* safely docked.

From a sailor's point of view I certainly regret that the company didn't keep using Fairlie, just a few miles further north - it was a much easier pier to work with. It seems the company didn't want to spend the money upgrading Fairlie and the Arran public preferred what they saw as the shorter (by 15 minutes) crossings to Ardrossan. Diversions and cancellations didn't seem to have entered into anyone's calculations!

The weather wasn't the only hazard lurking in the deep. The waters off Arran were also home to the infamous Perisher course - the Royal Navy's twice-yearly course to train its prospective submarine commanders, which also attracted candidates from other Navies across the world. It's so-named because, across a four-month period, it tests students to the limit in multiple scenarios and, if they fail to pass muster, it effectively signals the end of their career in submarines. Full stop.

It would seem that the deep water of the Arran Trench and the rapid changes of depth towards Ardrossan that make sea conditions so bad in rough weather actually provide the perfect, and most challenging possible training environment.

The Perisher course is not just famous for its rigour, with an average of 25% of candidates failing, but also for its rather

MV *Caledonia* through the cross-hairs being hunted down by the
Perishers (simulation)

brutal method of telling them they haven't made the grade. If someone fails the course, the first they'd know was when the submarine surfaced and they'd be swiftly removed by boat, or even helicopter. Their kit was already packed into the sea-bag by an unseen crew-member. No debrief, no appeal, just a rapid removal from the scene: and that would be the very last time they would ever set foot on an operational submarine.

The Navy had been using the area for decades so it was not that unusual for us to see one or two of our frigates engaged in cat-and-mouse exercises, or to see a couple of submarines on the surface after an exercise.

Even so, I must admit to being slightly alarmed one night in Brodick when I was shown a close-up photograph of me on the bridge of the MV *Caledonia* only a few hours earlier (the MV *Caledonia* was ex-Stena Baltica and a predecessor of the *Caledonian Isles*). We had been mid-passage from Ardrossan to Arran, and the photograph I was shown that night was crystal clear: quite unsettling that they could see such detail, and rather spooky to see myself bang in the middle of the cross hairs of the submarine's periscope sights. It certainly brought home to me what it must have been like on a convoy in the war mid-Atlantic: not a sign of trouble from horizon-to-horizon - and yet there we were - sitting ducks.

On further reflection, I suppose it must have been quite helpful to a beginner on the course to have their target ship working from a published CalMac timetable five times a day, and adopting the same route, day in, day out.

SHIP'S LOG
Still very much in CalMac service and on her original route: Ardrossan to Brodick.

STAR SHIP MV HEBRIDEAN PRINCESS
(FORMERLY MV COLUMBA)

Hebridean Princess country – Loch Na Lathaich, Mull - you can just make her out lying at anchor on the far left of the panorama (Bryan Kennedy)

NOT ACTUALLY A TRUE CLYDE VESSEL, REALLY MORE A WESTERN ISLES SHIP. NONETHELESS, I'VE INCLUDED HER HERE AS I WAS IN CHARGE OF HER A NUMBER OF TIMES OVER THE YEARS. FIRSTLY, WHEN SHE WAS STILL THE ORIGINAL CALMAC SHIP MV COLUMBA AND WAS USED AS THE RELIEF BOAT FOR ARRAN WHEN THE GLEN SANNOX WAS HAVING HER ANNUAL SERVICE, AND FINALLY WHEN SHE FIRST CAME INTO THE CLYDE IN HER NEW ROLE AND LIVERY AS THE HEBRIDEAN PRINCESS.

Hebridean Princess in the Kyles of Bute (Bryan Kennedy)

In the summer of 1994, just a few years after her multi-million pound transformation into the *Hebridean Princess*, she made her first visit to the Clyde. I was asked if I would be willing to go on her as Pilot for the week. I was nearing retirement from CalMac and the Marine Superintendent had recommended me for the role partly because I already knew her and partly because I was very familiar with the Kyles - and this had been advertised as a highlight of her trip. It turned out that the trip was also an informal job interview come practical exam and this led to a new and very enjoyable final phase in my career, as Relief Master of the *Hebridean Princess*.

The *Hebridean Princess* was the idea of Tony and Susan Binns. They had operated a successful canal cruising company in England for many years, but their own holidays were often spent as enthusiastic yachtsmen sailing around the Western Isles. It seems the concept came about when they found themselves stormbound one day in a sea loch on the West Coast and started discussing the idea of a possible new venture, taking people on mini luxury cruises to experience for themselves some of their own favourite scenic spots. At the time it was seen by most of the experts as a crazy idea, but with determination, some sound business sense and a clear knowledge of their target market, the Binnses unquestionably pulled it off.

All the time that they were in charge, they continued their annual sailing holidays and this informed the future itineraries. I can remember many a late-night discussion with them in Oban, awaiting a change of crew, discussing ideas for the future. They were passionate in their enjoyment of Scotland's unique scenery and in delivering for their clients, and it showed. Not really a Clyde regular, but she does have a full CalMac

Hebridean Princess (Martin Guppy/Hebridean Princess Cruises)

MV *Columba* (Michael Magnay)

Hebridean Princess in Loch Long (Captain Heaton/Hebridean Princess Cruises)

pedigree, and so I think she deserves at least an honorary place on my list. Rather than rank her I've given her five stars as befits her unique five-star luxury. She's also of course the only CalMac car ferry ever to have an inglenook fireplace in her main lounge!

FACT SHEET

- Built: 1964, Hall Russell, Aberdeen
- Entered service: 1964
- Left CalMac service: 1988
- Length: 235ft
- Tonnage: 1420 tons
- Speed: 14 kts
- Capacity: As the Columba, it was 870 passengers and 50 cars, now it's just under 50 guests, but in considerably more luxury.

VIEW FROM THE BRIDGE

As a small cruise vessel she is outstanding and very easy to handle: at least that is after the Binnses modified the rudder, tripling its effectiveness. Prior to that she and her two sister ships had 'devastated' the West Coast for nigh-on twenty-years – no pier remained unscathed.

The transformation from car ferry in my view is even more amazing when you realise that, when the ship was under construction, the Scottish Government designated the ship as a possible 'Emergency Centre of Government', one of three such 'citadel ships'. In reality, she was a floating nuclear bunker. The early sixties saw the height of the Cold War. The 1962 Cuban Missile Crisis, when the world seemed hours away from all-out nuclear war, had happened while she was still on the drawing board. US Polaris submarines, only a year or two earlier, had been first stationed at Holy Loch - where they were to remain for a further thirty years. And Britain herself was well on the way to building her own fleet of Resolution Class, missile-carrying nuclear submarines.

In addition to its normal role as a CalMac car ferry, the *Columba* and her sister ships (*Hebrides* and *Clansman*) were fitted with a number of additional facilities for her emergency role. Most of the measures were designed to combat possible radioactive fallout in the event of an all-out thermo-nuclear war. Measures included air-tight cargo-deck doors and bulkheads and an external, high-pressure water system to generate an all-enveloping water 'shield' to surround the vessel and deflect fallout. Internally she had decontamination areas, additional communications systems and massive deep freeze lockers to store enough food to feed her crew and VIP passengers for many weeks while the rest of us all fried.

Given this potential Cold War role, it's perhaps ironic that these days her only genuine connection with the state is her proudly displaying a Royal Warrant from the Queen as a 'supplier of luxury cruising': a fitting reward for becoming the de-facto replacement for the Royal Yacht *Britannia*.

I have wonderful memories of my time on the *Hebridean Princess*, not least looking at weather forecasts and scouring the charts trying to select the best anchorages in quiet, sheltered, scenic bays that we could reach by late afternoon each day. The itinerary was always fairly flexible, and it was at least as important to ensure our passengers could enjoy their gourmet meals in relative calm and have the opportunity for a pleasant night's sleep as it was to keep to the advertised itinerary.

The Captain's role in a ship like that is quite full-on however - not only do you have to do all the seamanship by day, but by night you also have to entertain the passengers at formal gatherings and at table. I'm pleased to say that I still keep in touch with one or two passengers who seem to have delighted in a few of my 'old salty sea dog' tales over the years.

Each itinerary was different, but irrespective of the route,

Hebridean Princess off Castlebay, Isle of Barra (Bryan Kennedy)

Reflections in the Kyles of Bute — *Hebridean Princess* (Bryan Kennedy)

one or two things were a constant. Firstly, every trip we received a dossier explaining all the dietary restrictions and requirements of each passenger in fine detail. And, every trip, they fastidiously kept to their required routine (low fat, lactose intolerant, gluten-free etc) - at least for the first night. But, two days in, the chef found they would almost all switch to his mouth-watering menu, regardless. Secondly, we could never have enough fresh water - there may have been only a maximum of 49 passengers on board, but they seemed to enjoy long showers and baths at any time of day. Consequently, we also had to add a stop or two to each weekly itinerary to replenish fresh-water tanks that were originally designed to keep the entire UK's Government alive for up to a fortnight in a post-apocalypse Britain!

She was a good sea boat and confidently makes trips across the North Sea to Scandinavia and the Baltic or out down the West Coast of Ireland on her varied annual programme. She also carries a list of VIP passengers as long as your arm, from Royals to F1 heroes, business moguls and celebrities, not to mention those just wanting an unforgettable, once in a lifetime, trip in stunning scenery.

SHIP'S LOG

Still going strong…

Hebridean Princess in Fairlie Roads, North Ayrshire with Arran Hills behind (Bryan Kennedy)

FINAL THOUGHTS

Looking back I am amazed at the variety of ships that I was Master on. From the old Clyde paddlers like the *Jeanie Deans* with 1,200 day trippers to the luxury mini-liner *Hebridean Princess*, with its 40 or 50 guests.

But it also makes me reflect on the reasons why people went on these boats in the first place and why they still have such fond memories. It's simple: the Clyde was a world-class holiday destination. That's surely as true today as it was then. People the world over, it seems, still want to enjoy views of the Clyde from the deck of a ship. Indeed it's interesting to note that in the summer of 2013, no fewer than 40 cruise ships of 10,000 tons or more visited the Clyde. Amongst that number was Cunard's flagship 150,000 ton RMS *Queen Mary 2* and her 4,000 passengers and crew.

It's great to think that the Clyde still exerts such a draw on people, especially when set against all the other sights, sounds and ports on offer worldwide. But it also pleases me to think that, even if it's only once a year, there is a new *Queen Mary* (RMS *Queen Mary 2*) carrying on the fine tradition of Clyde cruising of which I was part for so many years. Of course I also realise that, given her size, the RMS *Queen Mary 2* can never hope to offer the full 'Clyde' experience. She could never, ever, manage to follow her namesake on her old regular route through the Kyles and that, as I hope I have shown, will forever be her loss.

Thank goodness for the *Waverley*, only she can still deliver that true Clyde cruising experience and a trip 'Doon the Watter'.

HURRICANE HUTCH'S TOP 10 SHIPS OF THE CLYDE

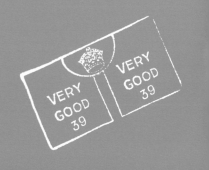